Landing Was The Easy Part

By

Edward Pappert

ISBN: 1-4033-2741-6 (e-book)
ISBN: 1-4033-2742-4 (Paperback)
ISBN: 1-4033-2743-2 (Dustjacket)

This book is printed on acid free paper.

1stBooks - rev. 10/23/02

Acknowledgements

Dr. Robert S. Pappert   My son Bobby is responsible for my writing this book. I wrote a book about how things were in the 20s and 30s for my grandchildren. I thought they would like to know about early radio, television, the great depression and what kids did back then. I wished one of my grandfathers had done this for me.

Bobby kept insisting I write about my war experiences. I wrote a few. Then my daughter Margie and my daughter in law Marta encouraged me to write more. With the help of a few friends this book resulted.

Ms. Helen (Misty) Coumbe   Misty is the widow of Vern Coumbe. She wrote the story of Vern's being shot down and spending the night on Japanese soil. Misty also typed many of the other stories that I dictated.

Glen Wallace   Glen flew with Vern and me. He also kept a diary of our daily missions. His diary and writings contributed greatly to the experiences and accuracy of this book.

Freddie Fox, Frank Thigpen, The Greek, George Minar, Art Hiser, Charles Hubenthal and others wrote of their experiences.

Mary Jayne   My wife made the book readable by insisting I explain many of the terms that were common to Navy Pilots but not to other readers.

All photos are personal photos, "Essex Air Groups CVG 83" copyright, 1946 by Air Group 83 book committee, unless otherwise noted.

Table of Contents

The War Years
Edward Pappert

Date of entry into active service: 11 November 1942

STC Slippery Rock, PA—Indoctrination
UNC Chapel Hill, NC—Pre Flight Training
Peru, IN—Primary Flight Training
Pensacola, FL—Flight Training

Commissioned Ensign 17 December 1943

NAS Jacksonville, FL Fighter training—
NAS Atlantic City—Air Group 83 formed—
Ayer, Mass.—Fighter Tactics F6F-Hellcat
Maui, (Puunnee) Hawaii-F4U Corsair

Boarded Carrier USS Essex 10, March 1945
Returned Home Seattle, WA 13 September 1945
Released to inactive duty—October 1945

Awards:
The Silver Star
The Distinguished Flying Cross
Seven Air Medals
American Theater Ribbon
Asiatic Pacific Ribbon-2 stars
Philippine Liberation Ribbon
Presidential Unit Citation

10 March 1945:

This is the Essex CV 9

Photo: United States Naval Aviation, 1910-1970 Dictionary of
American Naval Fighting Ships (Navair 00–50P-1)

Displacement	27,100 tons
	41,000 tons fully loaded as modified after WWII
Length	872 feet
Beam	147 feet 6 inches
Speed	33 knots
Crew	2,631

March the 11th:

Getting acquainted With The Ship

Today Air Group 83 boarded the Essex at Ulithi. I was assigned to a room. The room was on the hangar deck in the forward part of the ship. The plane at the front of the ship is on the Catapult. In case you don't know, the Catapult shoots the plane into the air. You feel like the stone in a sling shoot. I have three roommates – my wingman, Vern Coumbe, Glenn Wallace, and Clem Wear. Wallace, Coumbe and I fly together. We are flying with full Lieutenant James Stevens. We are fortunate to have a room. Many of the new pilots, or many of the pilots in our group, are assigned to one large area in the front of the ship. Our room is quite nice. As you enter the room, at the left hand side, there are two bunk beds. On the other side there are two beds. They are not bunk beds, but one of them is above the other following the outline of the ship, and that means you have to step over one to get to the other. I'm sleeping in the top bunk on the left hand side, with Clem Wear beneath me. There are two desks in the room, and two large closets and four chairs. The room has no door, it has a cloth curtain you push aside to enter. Just outside our room is a drinking fountain. And about thirty feet away there are showers. Living aboard ship is a nice way to fight a war. We put our laundry in a mesh bag every evening. It's picked up and brought back clean. Someone makes our beds.

While we're getting acquainted with the ship, we take a walk around. It is very, very large. There is a wardroom. The wardroom is where we have our meals. Our normal way of living is to return to our room after dinner, read and then play Acey-Deucy. (a board game played with dice-I believe it is the same as Backgammon) We make up teams, either Clem and I, or Vern and I, or Glenn and I play the other two. Those that lose go down to the wardroom at about midnight. They make a large stack of toast with cherry preserves and a sterling silver pitcher full of hot chocolate. Now remember, we're just 20-21 year-olds.

Later, after we get into combat and I become the division leader, we're given a fifth of liquor after combat missions. The first two times we brought the liquor back to the room, had a couple of drinks, but we didn't really like it. So after that we stopped taking the liquor. We could have taken it and sold or given it to sailors, but we didn't – we just didn't take it. It wasn't that none of us drank, we all drank, and fairly heavily before we went aboard ship. But being aboard ship and flying every day, liquor didn't seem to have any appeal to us. We preferred to have our toast and hot chocolate.

On the first night aboard while watching a movie that was shown on the hanger deck, general quarters sounded. No one told us about general quarter. It consisted of a series of loud gongs over the loudspeaker system. We were almost knocked over by the ships crew dashing to their battle stations. Two Kamikazes just dove on the fleet. One hit the USS Randolph a ship just behind ours.

No one thought a Kamikaze would come this far. That was the last movie shown on our tour of duty.

12 – 13 March:

Mog Mog Island, Beer in olive drab cans, and some unintentional swimming.

12 March:

We fly in groups of four. Our division is Wonder 21. Lt. James Stevens is the division leader. His wingman is Glen Wallace. I (Lt (jg) Edward Pappert) am section leader with Lt.(jg) Vern Coumbe on my wing. We were trained in the Hellcat (F6F) but switched to the Corsair (F4U) at the last stage of training. The Corsair squadron is designated as Fighter Bombing (VBF). The F6F squadron is designated as Fighters (VF). Both squadrons do the same things in combat and carry the same armament. (six 50 caliber machine guns in the wings, a 500 lb. bomb under the plane or 6 - 5 inch rockets).

The Corsair was a large plane as evidenced by the 22 pilots standing on the wing.

This Corsair caught a wire. However, he is still going to land hard.

The pilot did not walk away, but he survived.

13 March:

Squadron Insignia

Fighter Bombing Squadron 83 (VBF-83)

All squadrons had an insignia. This was ours.

The circles and lines in the background represent the gun sight that appeared on the canopy of the plane when the guns were turned on. They are orange as they were when turned on. The wings were gold.

The skull was white. This was created when we formed the Corsair squadron on the island of Maui.

Prior to the formation of the Corsair squadron our division was part of the F6F squadron. The dive-bomber squadron was drastically reduced in numbers and integrated into the F6F or Corsair groups. I believe this was done to create more fighter planes to counteract the new Japanese Kamikaze threat.

The insignia was reproduced in color on a vinyl patch that was sewn onto our flight jackets.

The F6F squadron's insignia had a Kangaroo with boxing gloves. No one cared for it, but Pug Southerland suggested it.He was our skipper. Everyone liked Pug Southerland. He was an Annapolis

Graduate. His executive officer Lt. Graham was also an Annapolis graduate.

He on the other hand was "regular navy" and wanted all of us non-ring wearers to know he was our superior. While in training at Ayer, MA, he decided all of the pilots should have other duties in addition to flying. I was assigned "Electrical Officer". My duty was to learn all about the electrical system of the F6F and give lectures to the rest of the squadron.

I went to an enlisted crew chief. He drew a diagram of the F6F's electrical system for me. My plan was to show the diagram to the squadron and tell them how to crawl out on the wing to unscrew the cowling around the engine and check the connections to the battery. Fortunately, before I was called upon to do this, results of our gunnery runs were made known. Gunnery practice consisted of shooting at a "sleeve" that was towed behind one of the planes. The 50 caliber shells in each plane were dipped in paint. We flew in groups of six. Everyone had a different color on the shells. Fortunately I had scored the most hits on the towed sleeve. I was now the "Gunnery Officer". My duties were to instruct those who did not score well in the art of shooting. I say it was fortunate as Lt. Graham was strictly G I. He would not have found my lecture on checking the electrical system while in flight the least bit humorous.

Lt. Graham was ambitious. When an opportunity came that allowed him to join a group at sea as a replacement pilot he jumped at it. No one was sorry to see him go. We were sorry to hear that he was shot down before we got into the fight.

14 March:

The Maui Party

We are underway, going into the warzone. During this period of time, or during re-fueling, we either do nothing, fly Combat Air Patrol, that is, flying above and around the fleet for protection, and/or just sit in a plane on the catapult. Today I was sitting in a plane on the catapult. You sit there for a couple of hours, and if you are needed for any attack you are immediately launched. In this case I just sat there. I did notice, however, in the instrument panel there was something missing. It was the clock. There's a nice clock with luminescent dials, about three inches across. It was missing from the airplane. Anyway, nothing eventful happened that day, I just sat in the plane waiting.

I almost forgot—in addition to flying combat air patrol, when we are re-fueling some of us are sent to a baby flattop to pick up replacement airplanes. When we leave we are given a parachute. We sit in what I think is called a breeches buoy; anyway it's a large basket with holes in it for your legs to stick out. They string ropes between the carrier and a destroyer. You sit in this basket and you are pulled across from the carrier to the destroyer, at which point you get out. The destroyer takes you to the baby carrier and you repeat the process. When we get to the baby carrier for the replacements, it's kind of nice duty because they usually have stuff like candy bars, which we don't have, so we can buy a supply of them. When we get there we must sign for the airplane, which is no problem, the Navy will lose the records anyway. When we sign we have to sign for a plane and a chute, we try to explain that we have a chute and don't need one. However, we are told that the airplane comes with a parachute and we must take the parachute. So we take the parachute. In the airplane you sit on the chute. In this case we have to sit on two chutes, which raises you about another four inches in the cockpit. This is usually no problem because the seat is adjustable. We fly back to our own carrier. When we land, we take the chute up to the parachute loft. We walk in and try to give it to the sailor on duty, he says, "I don't want the parachute, we've got more parachutes than we know what to do with." We take the parachute back to our room. By the time we got back to the fleet, we must have had eight or ten parachutes stacked in the room. But these were good, because we heard that the girls back home liked the chutes, they were nylon and they could make clothes out of them.

Jumping ahead, when we were coming back to Seattle, over the loudspeaker the Captain said, "If you go ashore with any Navy property not issued to you, you will be subject to court martial, and I don't think you want to spend the next few years in a Naval prison."

With that, we again tried to return the parachutes, and again they wouldn't take them, so all the parachutes got thrown overboard.

15 March:

The ships crew likes us. The brass on Maui where we trained didn't.

Our Air Group was to be the first group on the newest carrier, Shangra La. However we were sent to the forward area as a replacement squadron on the Essex. As it worked out this was a good move. The Essex had been operating for some time in the Pacific. The deck crew was experienced and all aboard knew their jobs well.

We were welcomed with open arms by the ships crew. Why? First of all those in the actual fighting felt that those who supplied the fighting fleet were not really in the war. Those in the supply fleet felt those back at Pearl Harbor were not as important as the supply fleet. Those at Pearl Harbor felt that those back in the states were somehow inferior to themselves. Those in the states felt that those not in the service were below them.

Why were we welcomed so enthusiastically?

The night before we left Maui we had a hellova drunken party. Two pilots decided to go back to state side so they drove a jeep eastward. They got about twenty feet into the Pacific Ocean. A truckload of us drove back to our quarters. Vern Coumbe was driving. He stopped to let a few jump off at their BOQ(bachelor officer quarters). Some one said OK, with this Vern started rather quickly. Twelve bodies fell off the back of the truck. They lay on the road. Gradually one by one by one got up. They say God protects drunks. He was working overtime that night.

Upon arriving at our quarters, we were faced with marines holding rifles over eight of our squadron. The black yeoman on duty at the front door was white. Seems he was sprayed with the fire extinguisher. Several pilots were shooting their pistols out the windows.

We went to Ulithi and boarded the Essex. Then we were assembled in the ready room. (This is the room in which we gathered before flights for assignments.) The skipper read a communication the ranking officer at the air station (Puunene) on Maui sent. After berating the entire group as the worst group ever to have been stationed at Puunene he went on to say "It is a court marshal offense to empty the fire extinguishers. Have the four offending officers shipped back to face a court marshal."

"Will the officers responsible please stand" said the skipper. Four pilots stood. I am going to ask again "Will those responsible please stand." The four said "We are standing". The skipper said "For the third and last time "Will those responsible stand". He then said "Well, I guess we will never know who was responsible".

The story of the party and the refusal to send the guilty back to Maui of course got around the ship. This endeared us to the enlisted men. Remember—those in the fighting fleet felt that those back on the island were "not really in the war".

The Essex was our home from March 10, 1945 till September 13, 1945. We should have been rotated back to the states in June, however we stayed. Either there were no immediate replacements or the powers to be knew of the atomic bomb.

Two Ensigns over Japan

Our first combat mission Vern and I (Pappert) are alone over Japan. We saw planes in a landing pattern. This would be like shooting fish in a barrel. We dove down and each shot a plane that was air born but in a landing attitude. Upon pulling up I saw three planes. Assuming they were part of our group we started to join up. Whoa, they were dull green with red circles (these were called red meat balls) painted on the wings. I opened fire on one. He turned right and climbed. Two bursts from the six 50 caliber machine guns and the next thing I knew I was flying through the debris of the Japanese plane. Completing the circle I saw a Japanese plane followed by Coumbe, he in turn was followed by another Japanese plane. I was behind all of them.

Was I keyed up? Vern Coumbe had been my wingman for at least six months. I started to call him on the radio. I called Hughie, then Sam (two of my best friends, with whom I went through training) before I called Vern. I said, "Let's get out of here." We climbed at full throttle to cloud cover. Then we started home.

As we neared the fleet we saw other Corsairs and joined them. They were part of the flight that we started with. Upon landing we found out that our division leader (James Stevens) was shot down by a Japanese plane. The squadron leader (Lt. Comdr. F. A. Patriarca) went to the wrong island and lost two of his four-plane division.

Thus the three of us (Coumbe, Wallace and I) became the utility group of the squadron.

We flew with our skipper (Patriarca-when he flew) and in F6F's when the Air Group Commander flew.

11

United States Pacific Fleet

COMMANDER FIRST CARRIER TASK FORCE, PACIFIC

In the name of the President of the United States, the Commander FIRST Carrier Task Force, Pacific, presents the AIR MEDAL to

LIEUTENANT (JG) EDWARD PAPPERT
UNITED STATES NAVAL RESERVE

for service as set forth in the following

CITATION:

"For distinguishing himself by meritorious acts while participating in an aerial flight as section leader on a fighter sweep over Kyushu, Japan on 18 March 1945. While engaged in combat with a superior number of enemy aircraft, he destroyed one enemy fighter. His skill and courage were at all times inspiring and in keeping with the highest traditions of the United States Naval Service."

M. A. MITSCHER,
Vice Admiral, U.S. Navy.

March the 19th:

The Franklin Gets Hit.

Ship's log[*] – 0330. Many bogies, several got through. Our gunners got one. The ship's planes are on strikes and sweeps against Kyushu and shipping at Kobe, a large naval base.

0445 – USS Franklin (carrier) was hit and burning furiously, with many explosions.

0745 – a Zeke (Japanese fighter) dove on us but missed. AA shot him down after dropping his bomb. Another tried but crashed in the water. Another dropped a bomb on us and headed for USS Bunker Hill. Our anti-aircraft got him. Our combat air patrol got two more. Strikes cancelled.

Our division - Bobcat 1 - was leading the groups on the strikes at Kobe naval base. Since our leader, James Stevens was shot down yesterday and the skipper of the squadron, Patriarca, lost two of his men, the three of us, that is, Vern Coumbe, Glenn Wallace and I, flew with the skipper. I flew second section leader with Vern on my wing and Glenn Wallace flew wing on the skipper. The Kobe naval base was a large naval base, with many ships at dock. It was a very hazardous mission, as the ships at the naval base were well-armed and we encountered a lot of anti-aircraft fire. After our dive, we headed back to the fleet. As we approached the fleet, we saw smoke. The smoke was quite thick and it looked like it was right in our path. When we got nearer, we found it was the Franklin, burning furiously and listing badly. We could see sailors jumping off the ship into the water. The Franklin was the aircraft carrier directly behind the Essex, so we got a Birdseye view of the damage done. We then landed aboard the ship with no further incident, and were just lucky that it wasn't the Essex that got hit.

---

[*] Entries made into a diary by a crew member

13

Ship's log – the Franklin is still burning and is dead in the water. At 1435 bogies closed. Our anti-aircraft got one. The Franklin is now being towed by the USS Pittsburgh (that is a cruiser, a ship larger than a destroyer). It's making only four knots. We were called to General Quarters – that means you're at your battle stations. We were there all day long, not secured, which means going back to your normal routine at 2000, that's eight o'clock at night. The Wasp an aircraft carrier in the field was hit and damaged, but not seriously. Air Group 83 got fifteen in the air and five on the ground. Yesterday they shot, nineteen on the ground and seven in the air today. Recap of damage to the enemy – Task Group 58 on the 19th got 75 planes on the ground and 75 in the air. Our losses, 22 planes. Air guns expended 575 five-inch shells - over 3000 40-millimeters and 3000 20-millimeters.

March the 20th:

Ship's log – 200 miles southeast of Kyushu. The Franklin reported still burning last night at 11 o-clock. One plane tried to dive on the Franklin, but missed. She's now making fifteen knots. Twelve planes attacked Task Group 58.2. Seven of them were shot down by Anti Aircraft fire. The Enterprise took another hit. The destroyer USS Paul took a bogie at 2100.

March the 21st:

Ship's log – 300 miles south of Kyushu. At 9 o'clock and 12 o'clock, two Bettys (twin-engine Japanese planes) were splashed by CAP (Combat air patrol). At 11 o'clock we went to General Quarters. Combat air patrol got six Frans (again, another Japanese airplane). Combat air patrol got a Betty attacking the destroyer DD Powers. Twenty-five Bettys closing with fighter coverage. Combat air patrol shot down a Myrt (another Japanese airplane), who was leading them in. We scrambled 36 fighters to take care of them, and they were intercepted at fifty miles. The Bettys were carrying two torpedoes and fighter torpedo bombers, probably suicide planes. None of them made it through to the fleet.

March the 22nd:

Ship's log – 600 miles from Kyushu.

Today our division (that is, Coumbe, Wallace and I along with a replacement ensign), were flying Combat air patrol over ships during re-fueling. We heard on the radio ships telling us they had spotted a bogie at 200 miles coming toward the fleet. We immediately took chase. Vern saw the enemy plane and motioned to me. We turned to make an attack – he was too far away to shoot. However, we were closing in on him and eventually would get to him. When we got near the fleet, however, we had another call from the Essex. This time they said, "what's your altitude?" We said we are at 10,500 feet. Again they called to us and said, "if that plane you're following goes into the clouds in front of you, don't follow it in". Now the clouds weren't that big, they were like big puffs, probably cumulus clouds, but they were I would say about a half-mile across. We did not follow it in, and we looked up and we could see an explosion, and the Betty came tumbling out in pieces. A five-inch gun from the Essex shot that plane in the cloud. The accuracy of that was just hard to believe. Nothing else of importance happened. We finished our combat air patrol and landed on the ship without further incident. Oh, yes, the plane I was flying in again was missing the clock.

USS Franklin (CV 13) showing extent of fires after hit by Japanese divebomber Mar 19, 1945. Franklin was attacked by a single Japanese plane which dropped two armor-piercing bombs, devastating the hangar deck and setting off ammunition. Casualties totaled 835 killed and 265 wounded.

Four plane comprised a division.
These were not from the Essex, as the tail marking is an S.

F 4 U The Corsair

Also known as:

Ensign Eliminator
The Hog

The Japanese called it:

Whistling Death

Corsair F4U Facts

Ask any pilot, Army, AirCorp or civilian what airplane they wished they could fly. One of the first or usually the first plane they would chose would be the F4U Corsair.

Why? The design is one answer. Those who knew more about it would say the performance.

When introduced, the Navy rejected the Corsair. Some said it could never be carrier based. It was dubbed "The Ensign Eliminator", as it was most difficult to land on a carrier. The plane was given to the Marines. The early version had a bad tendency to fall off to the left. This was corrected by putting a spoiler on the leading edge of the left wing.

The Corsair had two other names. The Japanese called it "Whistling Death". It was also called "The Hog". Why? The size of the engine and the very large propeller were the reasons.

We (Coumbe, Wallace and I) flew both the Hellcat and the Corsair. Both airplanes were tough. Both returned with holes big enough to throw a basketball through. The Hellcat was easier to fly. It was more forgiving. When landing on a carrier in a Hellcat, just cutting the throttle after receiving the cut resulted in a controlled crash. The tail hook caught a wire and the plane was slowed to a stop. I used this same technique the first two landings I made in a Corsair. Instead of crashing to the deck the Corsair floated nose up then caught a wire. The tail hook was pulled from the plane and the plane ran into the arresting wires. The arresting wires were steel cables raised off the deck to catch planes from plowing into those that had been brought forward after landing.

The Corsair had to be flown on to the deck. Oh, yes-to repair the torn tail hook from the plane required eight hours by two mechanics. We were in the war zone. The damaged planes were picked up by "Tillie"(our name for the crane) and dropped over the side.

One bad feature was the position of the pilot in relation to the front of the plane. The cockpit was way back, past the engine and the cooling system. Looking at the plane you would think there was no sense of balance. When flying this was not the case. The feeling was that the plane was part of you and it would respond to your every wish. The Corsair was fast. It climbed well. It responded quickly. It was a great airplane, but you had to fly it. It was a powerful plane.

Lt. R. A. Kinkaid   Ens. Ed Schiess   Ens. JoeEsherick

The Skipper "Ham Reidy" shows how he shot down the last Zero. This was on the way back to the ship. the war was supposedly over.

VBF
OFFICERS

ANDREW, Theodore L., Ens.	Amity, Pennsylvania
AUSTERMUEHLE, Edward W., Jr., Lieut.	Cleburne, Texas
BRADY, Raymond E., Lieut.	Darby, Pa.
BURR, Walter E., Ens.	Dover, New Jersey
CALHOUN, Finch W., Jr., Ens.	Oakland, Calif.
CALLAHAN, Glenn H., Ens.	Chico. Calif.
COUMBE, Vernon T., Lt.(jg)	Lombard Ill.
COMSTOCK, Franklyn M., Ens.	Columbia, S. C.
FARNSWORTH, William D., Ens.	Chandler, Arizona
FLANDERS, Robert C., Lieut.	Ypsilanti, Mich.
GILLUM, Robert L., Lieut.	Chico, Calif.
GODSON, Lindley W., Lieut.	Colonia, New Jersey
HARRIS, Grant, Lt. (jg)	Oak City, Utah
HARRIS, William P., Lieut.	Waldron, Arkansas
HILL, Mark L., Lt. (jg)	Yeadon, Pa.
HOOVER, Willard H., Lieut.	Canton, Ohio
ITEN, Ferdinand W., Ens.	San Francisco. Calif.
JACOBS, Harry, Lieut.	Jackson, Miss.
JETER, David M., Lt. (jg)	La Mesa, Calif.
JONES, Joseph W., Ens.	Salt Lake City 3, Utah
KANE, Arthur L., Lt. (jg)	Minneapolis, Minn.
KINKAID, Robert A., Lt. Comdr.	Washington, D.C.
KIRK, John E., Lt. Comdr.	Holdenville, Okla
KNAUS, Joseph, Ens.	Kansas City, Kansas
KUGLER, John C., Ens.	Salem, N. J.
LAMPRICH, Harry A., Lt. (jg)	Tulsa, Okla.
LAWRENCE, Luther D., Lieut.	Berwick, Maine
LEFEVRE, Adolphe C., Ens.	Philadelphia, Pa.
LILES, Raeford B., Ens.	Birmingham, Ala.
LLOYD, Harold A., Ens.	Dallas, Texas
MARCINKOSKA, John C., Lt. (jg)	Murphysboro, Ill.
McCLURE, Kenneth E., Ens.	Lincoln, Nebraska
McGOVERN, Thomas P., Ens.	Denver 16. Colo.

McLEOD, Kenneth A., Lieut.	New Hampshire
MILLER, John W., Ens.	Bakersfield, Calif.
MORRISSEY, Robert B., Lt. (jg)	Chicago, Ill.
NAGELL, Carl P., Ens.	Minneapolis, Minn.
PAPPERT, Edward, Lt. (jg)	Dormont, Pa.
PARISH, Rex o., Ens.	Ralls, Texas
PETERSON, Harry W., Jr., Lieut.	Red Wing Minn.
PORTER, William W., Ens.	Crookston, Minn.
RECHSTIENER, Roy O., Ens.	Los Angeles, Calif.
REIDY, Thomas H., Lt. Comdr.	Highland Park, Ill.
ROBERTS, George A., Lt. (jg)	Silex, Missouri
SAKELLARIADES, James C.,	Washington, D.C.
SCHIESS, Edward O., Lt. (jg)	Salem, Ore.
STAFFORD, Peary D., Lt. (jg)	Washington, D.C.
STRAUSE, Fred C., Lt. (jg)	Great Falls, Mont.
TEMME, Robert L., Lieut.	Kirkwood, Missouri
THIGPEN, Francis Y., Ens.	Greensboro, Alabama
TIGNOR, Carl M., Ens.	Richmond, Va.
TRIPP, Jack H., Lt. Comdr.	Riverside, Calif.
VALLELY, James L., Lieut.	West Roxbury, Mass.
WALLACE, Glen H., Lt. (jg)	Broseley, Missouri
WAY, Darrell E., Lieut.	Cody, Wyoming
WHITE, Francis R., Ens.	New Hampshire
WHITTEN, Homer W., Ens.	Jackson, Tenn.
WILCOX, Charles L., Ens.	Knoxville, Iowa
WOLFE, Tracy H., Lt. (jg)	Muncie, Indiana
WOOD, Harry W., Lt. Comdr.	Seattle, Wash.

23

VBF
Enlisted Men

Alsup, Grover C , AOM1c	Nashville, TN
Baker, Frank G, AMM2c	Grand Rapids, MI
Buss, George J , Y2c	Woodside, L I , NY
Campbell, Broodus E., ACMM	Greenville, SC
Casler, Dwyane L , AMM1c	Lansing, MI
Dowdell, Daniel D , ARM1c	Jackson Heights, L I , NY
Fritts, Raymond O Jr. AM1c	Casper, WY
Janiak, Anthony R ACMM	Pittsburgh, PA
Kramer, Marvin, AEM1c	Brooklyn, NY
Lapham, Robert H , PR2c	Andover, SD
Powers, Arthur L , Jr.,	London, KY
Reeves, John R , AOM1c	Chicago, IL
Schonborg, Hilton C., AMMP1c	Orland, CA
Shull, Charles B , ACRT	Modesta, CA
Wagner, Raymond O , ACOM	Newark, NJ
Zoubek, James, AMMH1c	Maple Heights, OH

The landing signal officer (Roy Bruninghaus) is showing one of us that his right wing is low. His arms represent the wings of the plane.

When the plane is level, the paddles will be straight out from his body. If the paddles go down to his sides, it means the plane is too low.

The LSO pictured here was well liked by all the pilots.

Edward Pappert

26 March:

Freddie Fox Escapes From Okinawa

Freddie Fox was a member of VF 83 when we were in Ayer, Massachusetts. He left our squadron early and joined Squadron number 9 at Maui.

Freddie's story was told to several of us at our reunion in Nashville, Tennessee on September 28, 2001. I recorded what I could remember. In the past Freddie would never talk about his experience. When he told the story, it was as though he was reliving the experience.

On March 26 anti-aircraft fire hit him when he was on a run over Okinawa. His plane was severely damaged. As he was coming down, his plane and another airplane collided. It took off his tail section and he got into a flat spin. (A flat spin is when your airplane is spinning instead of nose diving. The plane is straight and level spinning in a circle and losing altitude). Some other pilots called him and told him to bail out. He couldn't open his hatch to get out. He tried a side panel, which supposedly you could pop out, and he got stuck in that. He couldn't make his way out, so he kept trying to fly the airplane to keep it straight and level, and he succeeded in getting it to the ground. However, it hit rather hard, to the point that the only thing left was the cockpit. The wings were gone, the tail was gone, the motor was gone. The way he got out of the flat spin was that he had full throttle going down – and low pitch on the propellers.

Freddie then got out of the plane, (really the plane left him!) When he got out of the plane he saw some Japanese coming toward him and he ran over to a ditch and covered himself with hay or straw. The ditch was circled around a house. The reason for the ditch was that it was used to hold the water for the rice paddies. The Japanese would flood the paddies and it would keep the house from getting wet.

26

While he was in the ditch, one of the Japanese came over and saw him. Freddie stuck his gun in the Jap's stomach and shot him. The reason the others didn't hear it was because they were running around wildly shooting, so it was just another shot. He stayed in hiding in the straw until the Japanese left. He then decided he'd try to make it to the coast.

He was injured in the crash, particularly his left side, his right cheek and eye were severely damaged – I think his eyeball was partially out of the socket. He then crawled and made his way through rice paddies and sugar cane. Being an old farm boy, he understood some of these things, and he lived by eating anything that was green, and particularly the sugar cane. He stripped the leaves off the cane and chewed on the interior part. He found some caves that the Japanese had been using and he crawled into them to hide. He didn't know whether there were any Japs in there or not, but he went into them anyway.

He finally got himself to the coast. He knew from the plans of his carrier that we were going to bomb that particular coast, so he went clear to one end of it where he thought he'd be safe. He got into a cave that during high tide was under water, but at low tide he could hide. As he was trying to go from one cave to another, he saw a man carrying a lantern. There were some boats there, so Freddie crawled under one of the boats. He was about fifteen feet away from the lantern. The Japanese who was working the boats came over and turned his boat over, so Freddie was sitting there looking at the Jap. Again, he had his pistol with him and he shot the Japanese.

Then he took the boat turned it over and pushed it out into the water. The water was shallow at that point, so he pushed the boat out to get past the coral reefs. He had a long pole with him, and he got out past the reef and made one last push, and lost the pole! So now he's sitting all by himself in a boat. His fate depended upon the tides and the wind. At nighttime usually the tides come from the sea to the shore. However, the wind was strong enough that it took him a little bit further out to sea.

When he was out to sea, he had his life jacket with him, and some of the equipment. He dropped the yellow dye into the water. Two F4Fs (old Wildcats) came diving toward him. He thought they would strafe him, so he was waving his arms and his scarf., and apparently at the last minute they saw him and didn't fire.

They then proceeded to fly in circles around him until an OS2U (that's a float plane, which is catapulted from battleships or cruisers) came along.. The OS2U landed however, Freddie kept trying to keep them away because he knew there were coral reefs right beneath him. The plane landed and it did damage one of the pontoons, and it was taking on water. Freddie got into the OS2U, and they taxied out as fast as they could, but they couldn't take off because the pontoon was filling with water. The pilot was able, however, to get him to a ship that had been torpedoed and there was a rescue squad taking aboard survivors. Freddie got taken aboard the rescue ship and was then delivered to a destroyer. When he was taken aboard the destroyer, they wanted to give him morphine, but they didn't have any. However, Freddie had morphine with him from his survival kit.

After that he was out and didn't remember much until he woke up on the battleship where he had been transferred from the destroyer. On the battleship they put him into sickbay and tried to take care of his wounds the best they could. He was finally delivered to the island of Guam and from there, I guess, back to the States.

His name is Freddie Fox. It should have been Freddie the Cat because, as he said, there were at least four times when he should have been dead, but he survived.

28-29 March:

Two Corsairs overboard

Pilots man your planes.

We climb into our planes that are in the next to the last row on deck. I am second in from the right. Lt. (j g) Coumbe, my wingman is on my right. Lt. (jg) Art Hiser is behind us. The planes are staggered. Hiser is between Coumbe and me.

We are of course chained to the flight deck.

It is just starting to get light. It is raining and still quite dark. Time is about 5:00 AM. The first corsair takes off. The second one starts to roll down the deck. It's engine coughs. The pilot tries to stop. Over the side it goes into a gunnery station.

We are holding the brakes and revving the engines to full throttle. The plane chatters. The engine is going full speed. The chains and brakes hold the plane into position. I look back. Whoa—the backwash from Coumbe's plane and mine lifted Hiser's plane into the air and blew him off the fantail into the drink. A deck hand unchained his plane too soon. I call the tower. "Plane overboard I yell. We know answers the tower. The plane stuck in the cat walk but the pilot ejected and is in the water." No, I answer not the one taking off. There is one off the back of the ship."

Two small lights can be seen in the ocean. Both pilots got out and turned on the one cell light attached to their May West (inflatable jacket). Thank God for the tin cans (Destroyers). They picked up both pilots.

I am now signaled to the starters position and given the flag to take off. At the end of the deck my plane starts to settle toward the water. I do not go in. The plane manages to get air borne. I pick up the mike and yell "If you bastards want to see us all go into the drink move the starter up another 20 feet." (I could never understand why the starter didn't moves back some after the first row of planes took off.) The ship answers, "Who said that. It's against navy regs to swear on the air." They knew damn well who said it. But they were not about to take any action.

We were on a sweep to look for Japanese planes at or near Okinawa.

The flight was uneventful. That is except for the two pilots' that went into the drink.

28-29 March:

Ens. Art Hiser

Ens.Art Hiser was in the plane that got blown off the back of the ship This is what Art remembers.

Well, after I hit the drink, I can remember that I was under the water, and I got out of the cockpit and brought the chute with me. I swam toward the surface. It seemed like it took an awful long time to get there. When I got up, I got the raft out of the chute bag and got in it. When I first got up, I looked back at the carrier, and it had turned about 90 degrees from where I left it. After I got in the raft, I got the veri-pistols and shot off a couple of shots, and then I laid back in the raft and went to sleep, I guess, because it was after daylight when they picked me up. I was still good enough that I could climb up the ladder from the raft up to the destroyer. Then they took me in a medical room in there and gave me something or other, anyway it knocked me out. I wasn't awake for a few hours after that. I don't know, my memory wasn't too good then, and it's even worse now. I don't remember the name of the destroyer – I knew it then, but I don't remember it now. I didn't go back to the carrier. I was transferred from the destroyer to a battleship and I think it was the North Carolina. I was on the North Carolina and the South Dakota both.

I had eleven fractures in my jaws; one eye was out of the socket. So there was an awful lot of surgery and stuff before I got back together. The surgery was done on the battleship. I stayed out there with them until the other battleship was going back for some repairs, and they took me back to Hawaii to the hospital. I got back there about the first of June, I guess – the accident occurred late March – early April. Then I spent the rest of the war in the hospital at Texas Christian. The wounds are pretty well healed up, there are some marks on my face, but I don't have any trouble eating – I don't have any trouble doing anything.

1 April—Easter Sunday:

The Invasion of Okinawa

Strike on Okinawa in support of our invading troops. Lahey went down in flames from Anti Aircraft fire. Torpedo skipper made water landing. A Jap pilot landed on Yonton Airfield. A Marine shot him when he got out of the plane.

On this day the Allied forces invaded Okinawa. The invasion was to be made center island coming from the east. A mock invasion was made coming from the west at the southern tip. Most if not all of the Japanese forces were deployed to the southern tip. As a result there were few casualties upon landing.

We were given a map of the landing area that was blocked off into grids. Each of us had a specific spot on the map on which we were to drop our 500-pound bomb. Since the Japanese forces had been deployed to the southern tip of Okinawa all we did was blast holes in the sand. No enemy planes were sighted.

As our division leader had been shot down on our first mission and Commander Patriarca lost two of his division on that same mission Coumbe, Wallace and I flew with the skipper. As he was the head of the Corsair group we were first off on each mission.

The Japanese were fighting from an elaborate cave system they had created in the southern part of Okinawa. We carried 6 five-inch rockets. We would fly toward the hills and attempt to shoot the rockets into the caves. A number of our squadron landed on Okinawa. The pilots were taken by army jeep to the front lines. They were shown where our troops were and where the caves were located. The caves or the entrances were within 100 yards of our troops. They then flew over our troops and shot at the cave entrances.

After the first week Okinawa was considered a milk run. That is a very little enemy plane or ground fire was encountered. On the hops to Okinawa our skipper along with the three of us led the way.

However we would go to Kyushu about half the time. Here we would attack places like the Kuri Naval Base. On these missions we ran into intensive anti aircraft fire as well as enemy aircraft.

Commander Patriarca was always present for the Okinawa runs but when we went to Kyushu we were informed that he was having stomach problems. So, I (Lt (JG) Pappert) took over as the leader of the mission. After this happened numerous times I questioned the scheduling officer if this wasn't causing a problem. I was leading the mission when there were many officers of higher rank in the flight. He replied that no one came forward and asked to take charge and furthermore they felt I was doing an excellent job.

Several weeks later Commander Patriarca left the squadron and we were assigned a new skipper. He was Lt. Ham Reidy a nice guy and a capable skipper. Ham was a civilian pilot instructor who could have continued in that role for the duration of the war. He chose instead to become a naval aviator and get into combat.

From then on I was a division leader with Coumbe as my wingman, Wallace as second section leader and his wingman was anybody available. That is unless the Air Group Commander flew. Then, we flew the F6F. He was the leader with Wallace as his wingman and I had the second section.

Confidential OPNAV Report (Declassified)

CVG-83, Tactical and Operation Data

The accuracy and success of this attack is best indicated in the following quotation from the report of the Army ground forces on OKINAWA:

"Support NR 1 Essex with 4 VF and 12 VT bombed enemy troops and positions on reverse side slopes in target area 8172 3-4 and 8171 01-2. This strike was reported to have been the most successful of the campaign thus far in that it was the closest most hazardous mission yet attempted, with aircraft making their runs from south to north. Maximum distance from front was 150 yds up to extreme close quarters with no casualties resulting from aircraft. There was one 500 pounder which fell over ridge into our lines but fortunately this one was a dud and with no damaging results to our troops. This strike was so close it wiped out enemy troops who were on south side of the ridge throwing hand grenades over ridge into our own troops who were on north side of the ridge. There had been a briefing prior to strike and an Army liaison officer was flying with the flight leader to lead them into target area. On prior missions in an attempt to take this ridge the Army reported that over 325 casualties resulted. With this particular strike there were 2 ridges taken by ground troops immediately after completion of the strike with only 2 casualties resulting and those caused by ground action. 24th Corp from General Hodges to front lines were very well please and satisfied with results and accuracy that pilots displayed in their drops."

(Narrative)   VBF-83

This support mission was launched from the Essex and landed at Kadena Field, Okinawa for special briefing. Target assignment was an enemy strongpoint full of caves and pits on the south side of a 300-foot hill. Our troops had advanced to the top of the hill but the southern side was so steep and so located that the enemy positions (caves) could not be reached by artillery fire. Our troops had been stalemated in this position for a period of about three days and had experienced a great number of casualties (estimated 325) in attempting to take this position.

The regimental commander of our units concerned had consented to use air support in this instance as a last resort. His reasons for reluctance to use this method previously were: (a) location of the "pocket" necessitated dives by our planes toward our own forces; and, (b) our front lines were a minimum of 50 yards away. It was so planned that on completion of our attack, friendly artillery would open up and our infantry would storm the position.

Our planes were loaded with delayed action, 500# GP bombs and the briefing called for VBF planes to drop between the first and second runs of VT. On completion of the bombing, VBF was to retire some 1000 yards to the south and strafe positions from Shuri to Yonabaru, making their runs from west to east to avoid artillery and mortar fire.

The attack was carried out with an 800 to 1000 foot ceiling prevailing and bomb drops were made at about 400 feet (100 feet above the ground). All bombs were placed squarely in the enemy positions and the comment made from the ground was "excellent, if we don't take the hill now we never will."

VBF planes carried out the strafing mission, as scheduled, on completion of the bombing, causing a small fire and damage to positions assigned.

It is believed this was the closest support carried out to date and the fact that the attack had to be made in the direction of friendly forces, under adverse weather conditions, combined with the results achieved, gained a tremendous amount of confidence and gratitude from the ground forces in regards to air support in general.

VT-83

Essex planes landed at Kadena, and were briefed there by the support leader, Lt.Cdr. Stewart, on photos and intelligence material made available by Marine and Army ground officers for this strike. The target was the southern slope of a hill northwest of Yonabaru which strongly entrenched enemy forces had been holding for over a week.

The eight VT planes dropped their 32 x 500# GP's on enemy positions which extended to within 50 yards of our own lines, wiping out the enemy troops and emplacements without injury to friendly forces. Our ground forces advanced immediately after the attack and suffered only two casualties in an area where 325 casualties had been inflicted in previous attacks.

An unusual feature of this support was the radical tactics of diving directly towards out own lines, requiring precise bombing in order to prevent injury to friendly troops. Because of the steep reverse slope on which the enemy had dug in, it was necessary to "throw" bombs into their positions by diving towards and pulling out over our own forces on the opposite slope.

2 April:

Two Typhoons in the area.

Even though the Essex was a very large ship. It was just like a cork on the ocean. While lying in our bunks, we could feel the ship go down twice, then it would come up three times. It continued like this all night long.

3 April:

Lt. Gunner Way went into the drink. He was rescued.

5 April:

Flash back

Unless it was a case of "Navy Needs", the navy gave cadets their choice whenever a choice had to be made. The class was ranked top to bottom according to achievements. Mostly this was based upon our scholastic standing.

After pre flight, some of the choices were: what E Bases to go to, type of training i.e. twin engine, fighters, lighter than air or torpedo bombers.

Just before we were to be commissioned officers, a Marine Colonel addressed us. He said that 20% of us were to be marines. He said the marines want the best.

As was the navy's way, the first in the class was asked if he wished to be a marine. After going through the whole class, the marines got about half of their needs. A second talk by a Marine General got a few more. Then the Navy Commander said, "When we face a situation like this, we go in reverse. He started at the cadet who finished last and continued in this order until the marine quota was filled.

Several of our friends were asked why they chose the marines. Most of them said they were afraid they could not navigate well enough to find their way back to the carrier.

5 April:

Four marines joined our squadron. They were replacement corsair pilots. I knew one of them (O'Neil) from flight training.

In searching for the Japanese fleet, my division was given the assignment to relay any sighting of the Japanese fleet back to the

Essex. My wingman and I took two of the marines as our second section. Wallace and his wingman took the other two marines as their second section. I was to fly 400 miles toward Japan. Wallace and his division were to orbit 200 miles from the ship. We were to orbit at the highest altitude we could. Others went out on a search pattern. If they sighted the fleet they were to radio me. I in turn would relay the message to Wallace's division. They would relay the position to the Essex. Upon reaching our position outcropping of rocks could be seen. They were just south of Japan. We were able to climb to 40,000 feet. (This was 3000 feet above the rating of a corsair). We held this position for 3 or 4 hours then returned to the ship.

This was to be repeated the next day. The four marines wanted to fly as a division. They were given the assignment to take the position I had the previous day.

A good friend of mine, Jack Lyons, sighted the Japanese fleet the next day.

The marine division failed to return to the ship at the expected time. I went to the control room. There was a large circular screen on which the aircraft showed up as a lighted blip on the screen. We could see where they were. They had been blown off course about 300 miles. We could hear them talking to one another. The ship would not contact them for fear that the Japanese could locate our fleet. (At an altitude of 40,000 feet it seems there is no air. The planes controls had little effect. Winds at this altitude could be in excess of 100 mph).

Knowing they were about to run out of gas they decided that the first one to do so would land in the water. The others would drop their life rafts near him. We carried small life rafts under the seat of the planes. Then the others would land close to him. From the air the second and third to land could be directed by the plane in the air diving over the pilots in the direction of the others. This worked fine except one was killed in landing.

How did we know this happened? We got a letter from the three marines about three weeks later. It was post marked from San Diego.

It is hard to believe but one of our submarines saw them landing. The chances of this are about the same as winning the state lottery. They were picked up and returned to the Hawaiian Islands.

Did I say Marines couldn't navigate? Maybe I was wrong. They found their way back to the states months before the rest of us.

6 April, 1945:

TWO SUBMARINES

My squadron (Coumbe, Wallace and a replacement Ensign) was orbiting over Naha Base at the southern eastern end of Okinawa. We were on patrol, and were to orbit this position until relieved (about 4 hours later).

The naval ground control station was Boxthorne Base. Our squadron, for this Mission was called Boxthorne 1. Through the radio we heard:

Boxthorne base this is boxthorne 1 —over

Boxthorne 1 this is boxthorne base —over

Boxthorne base I am circling at 20,000 feet directly above you. Do you see me? —Over

Boxthorne 1 I see you —over.

About 15 minutes later

Boxthorne base this is boxthorne 1. I see a submarine following a small ship just off the harbor. —Over

(Excited voice) Boxthorne 1 go lower and investigate —over

Circling lower to 5,000 feet

Boxthorne base there are two submarines (Periscopes) following that ship. Both are about 50 feet behind and at 45-degree angles —over

(New voice) Hey Pappy, What kind of a sailor are you? Those are paravanes. That is a tug clearing the harbor of mines. —over and out

When we went to the Philippine islands in June for a two-week rest I heard that story from several of my friends who were stationed aboard other carriers.

CAG Commander H.T. Utter, USN

Commander Utter was a nice guy. We only saw him when he flew.

He flew the Hellcat (F6F),which was not too often. When he did, Lt. Glen Wallace was his wingman, I (Lt.(jg) Ed Pappert flew as his second section and Lt.(jg) Vern Coumbe as my wingman.

STAFF OF COMMANDER AIR GROUP 83

Back row: Lt.(jg) R.L. Pierce, Lt. H.F. Bennett, Lt.(jg) H.B. Powers
Front row: Comdr. H. T. Utter, Lt. Comdr. W. H. Walker, (MC), Lt. Comdr A. K. Bell, Lt. Buyoucos, Lt. F.R. Sullivan

Enlisted Personnel:

W.H. Dwiggins, ARM1C   G.E. Zimmerman, ART1C
H.L. Dollard, CPHOM   L.G. Dibb, ART1C
W.H. Nortz, ART2C   R.A. Kimball, Y1C
D.J. Beaupre, AMM3C   W.H. Delezenne, ARM3C

Edward Pappert

Photo # 80-G-59314 F6F-3 fighters landing on USS Enterprise after strikes on Truk, Feb. 1944

Photo: Department of the Navy Naval Historic Center
Washington D.C.

This picture shows how the wings of a Hellcat Fold, to save space
aboard ship.

7 April:

CDR Utter coordinates the attack on the Yamato.

Glenn Wallace kept a diary. I quote from that diary:

"7 April (1945)—We finally found the Jap fleet, (Jack Lyons first to spot it). We sank the Battleship Yamato, 2 Cruisers and 4 destroyers. The Air Group shot down 10 planes and the Essex was under attack all day. The Hancock was hit by a Kamikaze and 30 killed. We lost all four of the Marine Corsair replacement Pilots. One Dive Bomber lost."

"During the Yamato strike, Pappert, Coumbe and I (Wallace) flew with El Groupo, (CDR Utter), while he coordinated the attack on the Yamato. Had a ringside seat at 3000 feet for the whole show. Saw one TBM launch his torpedo and it porpoised right into the side of a Jap destroyer - blew it all to pieces". When all the attacking planes had headed for home, the Battleship was sinking and the Cruisers and Cans were on their sides. At this time our leader said "Hey Guys, lets go in and get a hit on them". So, in we went until suddenly a solid curtain of AA fire confronted us. I believe the Jap crews of the crippled ships were even firing rifles and they had only one target, us. Anyway, CDR Utter then had a better idea; he said "lets forget that run and do a 180", which we did and dropped our bombs for a direct hit in the Pacific Ocean. (We flew those Hellcats 5 ½ hours on that hop)."

The Japanese battle ship
"The Yamato"

The Japanese battleship Yamato was sunk in 1945 while on a desperate mission to turn the tide of the Pacific War. The Yamato was one of two 72,800-ton battleships which were the largest ever built. She had nine18-inch guns, which could hurl shells 25 miles.

After seeing action at Midway, the Solomon Islands, Truk and the Philippines, the Yamato was kept mostly in port at Kure, near Hiroshima. The sister ship Musashi was sunk by carrier-based planes in the Battle of Leyte Gulf. The big battleships lack of speed hindered them from serving as escorts for carrier forces.

During the battle for Okinawa in April 1945, Japanese officers decided to use it for a final sortie that might help turn the fighting in Japan's favor by beaching the giant ship and using its giant guns against U.S. land forces. On April 6, 1945, the Yamato sailed from Tokuyama, on Japan's Inland Sea, with just enough fuel for a one-way voyage. The next day the battleship and its escort flotilla - a light cruiser and eight destroyers - were attacked by 380 planes from U.S. Rear Admiral Marc Mitscher's Task Force 58.

An ESSEX Hellcat flown by Ensign Jack Lyons of VF-83 found them within range. It was 8:22 A M "one Yamato-class battleship, one or two cruisers and eight destroyers…"

"Pilots, man your planes!" Avengers, loaded with torpedoes: Helldivers, with semi armor-piercing bombs, and fighters with 500-pound bombs took off at 10:00AM. The entire striking force of Task Groups 58.1 and 58.3 was aloft. Task Group 58.4 followed 45 minutes later. In all 386 planes streaked northward.

Planes from two task groups of 58 were closing fast. Lieutenant Thaddeus T. Coleman of VF-83 tells what happened: "It was a dull flight and as usual nothing to do. I smoked and then smoked some more; chewed a couple packages of gum and finally began to count planes. We were in such a compact formation that it was easy...50, 75...150...200...250, and I quit counting. It wasn't safe. I had just turned to count the planes to my right and saw an F4U (Corsair) spin dizzily out of a cloud, his tail assembly clipped away by a collision. I quit counting.

A bomber pilot radioed, 'I'm over the target location, where are the Japs?' "That was the last communication that I remember. Slowly our radios had developed a whining sound, which grew worse, and worse. The Japs had jammed our voice communications. Rain and more clouds. We couldn't see or hear.

There was a sudden eruption of AA close ahead. Then we knew we had found them and because of their bursts, we knew where they were. Naturally we scattered, to begin the most confusing air-sea battle of all time. The Japanese gunnery officers were handicapped because they didn't have the slightest idea from where the next attack would develop. Nor did we, the attackers, for that matter.

"Our training instructions, to dive steeply from 10,000 feet or higher, proved useless. Here the ceiling was only 3,000 feet, with rainsqualls all around. Bomber pilots pushed over in all sorts of crazy dives, fighter pilots used every maneuver in the book, torpedo pilots stuck their necks all the way out, dropped right down on the surface and delivered their parcels so near the ships that many of them missed the ships' superstructures by inches.

The first strike came in two big waves. The first scored four bomb hits in the vicinity of No.3 turret, just aft of the bridge, and two or three torpedo hits on the port side. The bombs started a fire, which was never extinguished. The second wave of (torpedo) planes scored several hits on one side of the battleship, causing her to list heavily to port. Then, a few moments later, planes from the opposite side scored equally as many hits, and the heel to starboard put her on an even keel. It is doubtful if damage-control officers aboard Yamato could have done as well. Speed was reduced from 28 knots to 18. Later in the action, the Yamato listed heavily to port. Her massive armor belt on the starboard side could be seen high out of the water, exposing her more vulnerable underbelly.

The final blow…six Yorktown torpedo planes. All made perfect runs; so did at least five of the torpedoes. Her bottom ripped out, pushed over by the tremendous force of the underwater explosions, Yamato slowly rolled on her beam ends. Billowing sheets of steam, flame, and spray veiled Yamato's departure.

The smoke cloud billowing thousands of feet was seen by coast watchers on Kyushu more than 100 miles away.

Of its crew of 3,300 only about 260 survived.

Also acknowledge the contributions of Ray Atwell for the Yamato story. Ray was in CIC at this time.

Everyone watching preparations for a flight have seen the pilots carrying their chart boards to the plane and insert them in the tracks that ran underneath the dash.

Now, the pilot has finished his mission of bombing or strafing or a dogfight and it is time to head back to the carrier. How do you know where you are and what direction to fly to get back to the ship? It is not as simple as flying West and then heading back east. Besides that the carrier has moved in the meantime!

Finding the ship

Navigation was one of the major studies we had while we were cadets. It was one of the main reasons cadets chose to become Marines.

All of us carried a plotting board. The plotting board was a writing surface with a clear plastic cover mounted on a metal frame. The metal frame was about twenty inches square. A grease pen was used to draw on the plastic surface. This slid under the instrument panel...

During the briefing prior to every hop, we were given the compass heading to the target. We were also given the ships heading, the ships expected speed, the wind velocity and direction. From this we would plot our heading and calculate our speed to determine our position when we were at the target. If we changed direction and or flew longer than planned we could calculate our new position.. There was a moveable compass on the plotting board that would turn. This enabled us to determine our heading home.

Of course the ship occasionally changed course as did the wind.. This information was never broadcast. Sounds complicated? Not really. From our original plotting we knew the heading home before we started. This was usually all we needed. Changes in targets that resulted in course changes could be recalculated.

There were times when the target was changed, the ship changed course, as did the wind. If there weren't another factor many pilots would have been lost at sea. The other factor was the radio. Letters of the alphabet would be sent from the ship at about every ten degrees of the compass. Prior to leaving the ship we were given the code. If the letters m- o- n were broadcast from the ship at 170-180-190 degrees, the reciprocal of the center letter would be taken. In this case it would be 90 degrees. If the letters changed to opq, then the heading would be corrected to 100 degrees.
The radios were reliable most of the time.

George Minar, a hellcat pilot, sent me his experience on the strike against the Yamato.

April 7, 1945

When Jack Lyon's Division returned to the Essex, after locating the Japanese fleet, pilots were hastily scrambled to track the fleet. Due to a knee injury, I was temporarily grounded and missed going with the main group. However, shortly after they left, I received permission to participate, and my division took off.

Based on Jack Lyon's report, we were able to locate the fleet. The visibility in the area was very poor with considerable cloud cover and an extremely low ceiling.

During that time, my wingman, Jack Farrell, spotted a very low flying plane, which turned out to be a twin engine Sally. We immediately gave chase, and I shot it down. Having lost contact with the fleet, we had to resort to doing a square search. Flying just off the surface, we ran into heavy fog, and, shortly afterward, I could see a series of bright orange-colored flashes. In a matter of seconds, I saw a dark gray silhouette forming, which turned out to be the Yamato.

Talk about surprise, we were just seconds away from becoming unintentional American Kamikazes. We had to drastically reduce speed to the point where we dropped our flaps and landing gear as we executed over ninety degree turns, to avoid crashing into Yamato's hull. Two of our planes turned hard port, and my wingman and I turned starboard. Believe me, we spared no power to get to a safe altitude.

From there on, we maintained minimum flight speed to save fuel and keep visual contact with the fleet. Yet, so desperate were the Japanese, they dispatched one destroyer to try and shoot us down. Shortly afterwards, I was contacted by the attack group that now had the fleet in sight, and we were ordered to return to the Essex. To this day, I don't know how we managed to slip through their destroyer screen. Incidentally, the bright orange flashes we saw were apparently from their heavy guns firing into the ocean to create water barriers in hopes we would crash into them.

7 April:

Jack Lyons finds the Yamato

Charles Hubenthal was a F6F pilot who adds this:

Our squadron leader Archie Sturdivant did not get off on that hop so Jack Lyons led Joe Warrior and I. The ceiling was about 3000 feet with clouds up to 12,000 feet. Jack saw the Japanese fleet first. He radioed the information to the ship.

Years later our son was in the navy with Sasebo, Japan as homeport. He met and married a Japanese girl. He found out later that his wife's father went to school with the daughter of the captain of the Yamato. Our son Chuck lives in Tokyo and teaches English as a second language. They have two children, a boy and a girl. We visited them a few years ago and met his wife's parents.

The Avenger TB

The VT squadron flew the TBM. This torpedo plane was big and carried a large torpedo. The F6F (Hellcat) squadron and the F4U (Corsair) squadron planes accompanied the Torpedo Bombers to protect them on their missions. They had a gunner on board, but their slow speed and lack of maneuverability made them vulnerable to attacks by enemy fighters.

However, if the objective was to sink ships, nothing could do the job as well as torpedoes.

As fighter pilots we did not envy the torpedo pilots. Their job was to fly straight at the enemy ship and launch their torpedo when they were very close. The enemy ships concentrated their firepower on the attacking torpedo planes.

During the attack on the Yamato, I watched a TBM drop its torpedo then fly directly into the hull of the Yamato.

Lt.(jg) James Boatright was killed 20 May, 1945. He was a Torpedo Pilot everyone knew and liked.

V T
Officers

Bass, Russell J. Lt (jg)   Grand Rapids, MI
Barrett, William E. Lt (jg)   Brookline, MA
Beeson, Donald R. Lt.   Hutchinson, KA
Brown, William A. Lt.   Huntsville, AL.
Byrne, Paul V. Lt.   Chicago, IL

Cabell, John B. Lt. (jg)   Glasgow, MT
Giles, John W. Ens   Fuquay Springs, NC
Hamor, Robert B. Lt.   Northumberland, PA .
Hervey, Robert W. Lt. (jg)   Denver, CO
Hodges, Eugene W Jr. Lt. (jg)   Reynolds, GA
Jacobs, Linus G. Lt. (jg)   Gorham, KA

Johns, Harry E. Lt. (jg)   Denver, CO
Ker, Richard W, Lt. (jg)   Ririe, ID
Leclair, Dewey I. Lt. (jg)   Seattle, WA
Lewellen, Lloyd C. Lt.   Colombia, MO
Nicholson, Robert H Lt. (jg)   Chattanoga, TE

Palermo, Carlo Lt. (jg)   New Orleans, LA
Plant, Roy U Lt.   New Haven, CT
Roe, Joe D. Lt.   Longview, TX
Shrauger, William H. Lt. (jg)   Buffalo, NY
Shumway, John E. Lt.   Pleasant, KA

Sleepeck, William H. Lt.   Oak Park, IL.
Stewart, Henry A. Lt.Comdr   San Juan Capistrano, CA
Suggs, Hubert D Ens.   Summerland, MS
Walden, James W Lt   Wrens, GA
White, Henry C. Lt. Comdr   Hingham, MA

VT ENLISTED MEN

AKERS, Arthur O., ARM1c	Indianapolis, Ind.
BAGNE, Arthur L., AMM2c	Gonvick, Minn.
BARCZYS, Edward A., AMM1c	Buffalo, N. Y.
BENESKI, John T., AOM2c	Olyphant, Pa.
BOWMAN, Henry L., ARM2c	Columbus, Ohio
BRADBURY, Arthur B., ARM2c	Stratford, Conn.
BRAY, Ulmon C., ARM2c	Shawnee, Okla.
BRESSON, Lawrence G., AOM3c	Wooster, Ohio
BRIDGES, Ezra J., ART1c	Camp, Miss.
BROOKS, Roy, Jr., AMM3c	Bardstown, Kentucky
CONONICA, Frank G., ARM3c	Englewood, N. J.
CHASE, Richard A., AOM3c	Merrimac, Mass.
CROUCH, Howard L., AOM2c	Long Beach, Calif.
CULLER, Wayne R., ARM1c	Eureka, Kansas
DENNY, Everett C., AOM1c	Winston-Salem, N. C.
DONLEY, Edward J., AOM1c	Holland Patent, New York
EAGAN, John G., AMM3c	La Porte, Indiana
EBERHART, John R., ARM2c	Fullerton, Calif.
ENGSTROM, John J., ARM3c	Rawlins, Wyo.
EVANS, William P., ARM3c	Kaysville, Utah
FAHRENHOLZ, Robert C., AMM3c	Alexandria, Ohio
FITZGERALD, Joseph L., AOM2c	Lynn, Mass.
FOTI, Peter J., AMM2c	Astoria, L. I., N. Y.
FULLER, Frank V., ACEM	Milwaukee, Wis.
GATTUSO, Frank, AMM3c	Paulsboro, N. J.
HEATH, Charles C., ARM1c	Olney, Ill.
HUDDLESTON, Dick H., PR1c	Redondo, Calif.
JOHNSON, Kenneth O., AMM3c	New Britian, Conn.
JOHNSON, Paris W., ARM3c	Angie, Louisiana
JONES, Robert L., AMM1c	North Lima, Ohio
JONES, Twyman D., ARM3c	Greenville, S. C.
JOSLIN, Merrill A., ARM3c	Kansas City, Mo.

55

KELLIHER, Elmer E., ARM2c	Holyoke, Mass.
KENDALL, James O., AMM2c	Shillington, Pa.
KISSLING, Lawrence J., Y1c	Roslyn, New York
KOSTYK, Gordon, ARM3c	Campbell, Ohio
LASOTA, Walter, Jr., ACMM	Jacksonville, Fla.
LATZKO, Gordon C., AMM2c	Ridgefield Park, N. J.
LEDBURY, Donald J., ARM1c	Troutdale, Oregon
LICATA, Salvatore W., AMM3c	Lockport, N. Y.
LILLARD, James W., ARM3c	Phoenix, Ariz.
MAIZE, Brooks R., ARM2c	Longmont, Colo.
MARTIN, Edwin L., ARM1c	Elsinore, Calif.
McFARLAND, Earl G., AOM1c	Ode Bolt, Iowa
MOON, Henry A., AOM1c	Richmond, Va.
PAKIS, James, AMM3c	Brooklyn, N. Y.
PAUL, John M., ARM2c	Kansas City, Mo.
PETERSON, Earle S., ARM3c	St. Paul, Minn.
PURTELL, James P., ARM1c	Somerville, Mass.
QUINN, James E., AMM1c	Fall River, Mass.
RAINEY, Irving C., AMM3c	Prospect, Maine
REGNER, Harold I., AMM3c	Austin, Minn.
RICHERT, Morris A., ACMM	Murdoch, Nebraska
SANCHEZ, John J., AMM3c	Chicago, Ill.
SANDERS, Elwood L., ARM2c	Tulsa, Oklahoma
SCHMIDT, Edward F., AMM3c	Milwaukee, Wis.
SMITONICK, John, AMM2c	Bayside, L. I., N. Y.
SNYDER, Joseph E., AEM2c	Beaver Falls, Pa.
TIPTON, William O., AMM3c	Covington, Ky.
TRAVERS, Robert L., ARM2c	Peoria, Ill.
TURNER, Frederick A., AMM1c	Dorchester, Mass.
VIGLIONE, Walter A., AOM1c	Revere, Mass.
WHITE, Daniel F., AM1c	Philadelphia, Pa.
WILLS, Robert J., AMM3c	Port Clinton, Ohio
YOUNGBLOOD, James H., AMM3c	Farmington, Ohio

Torpedo Bomber with folded wings
The mechanism that permitted this added weight
but was necessary to save space aboard the carrier.

The war ended so everyone flew past Mt. Fuji. Most Corsair and Hellcat pilots did a slow roll with Mt. Fuji in their gun sights. I don't think the TBM or The SB2C (dive bombers) did or if they could.

If any of them did, I am sure they will tell me about it.

The TBM carried a torpedo. If sinking ships is your mission, nothing compares to this plane.

Of course to do this, the pilot flies right above the water and directly at the target. It is almost a suicide run as the ships gunners can shoot directly at you.

When we attacked the Yamato, I watched one of our torpedo planes fly straight into the side of that Battle Ship.

This is the type of airplane that President George Bush flew.

12 April:

Glen's log—

Worked over Okinawa. Air Group shot down 13 Japs today. We are now short of F4U's so Pappert, Coumbe and I are flying F6F's.

We were also short of pilots. Both planes and pilots were replaced. One of the replacement pilots was Frank Thigpen. Frank recalled his experience of joining Air Group 83.

FIRST FLIGHT
by
Frank Thigpen

I will never forget the first time I saw the carrier Essex. I came aboard by "highline" from a destroyer off Essex' port quarter, on to the stern as there was a tanker along the starboard side. There was about 8-10 of us coming aboard as "replacement" pilots. Those of us flying F4U Corsairs were assigned to VBF-83.

We spent the first day getting squared away, like finding the head, living spaces, the wardroom, the Ready Room, etc. The next day we checked out some of our flight gear and spent quite a bit of time in the ready room listening to the briefings of outgoing flights. We had been told that we would not be scheduled for several days, which would give us more time to get adjusted to everything. However, that morning, 16 April 1945, we were about to go down to the wardroom for early chow when the Flight Schedules Officer approached and said he was sorry, but it would be necessary for two of us new pilots to fly that afternoon. Several planes had been shot down and they were sending out rescue flights and we were to provide the fighter cover. Well, after many flips of the coin, Ensign Francis White and myself were selected to be part of the Res Cap flight. We quickly had lunch and returned to the ready room with our flight gear.

After suiting up and inserting the proper templates in our plotting boards, we all sat down for the briefing. The briefing officer told us that two or more planes had been shot down on the morning raids over Kanoya, on the southern end of the island of Kyushu. They were seen to have crash-landed in Kagoshima Bay and believed to have gotten out of their planes. The Task Force Commander had directed a Dumbo (PBY) be sent to that area and since it was in enemy territory, we were to provide the fighter protection.

In due time our briefing was over, including the Flight Leader's comments. He stressed that we would be operating quite close to one or more Japanese airfields and for each of us to keep a sharp lookout. We left the ready room and hit the flight deck on the double. Found my F4U with it's "double diamond" on the tail. She was different from the Corsairs I had flown previously. First, she had a large 150 gal. belly tank for estra endurance. Also, all the 50 caliber wing guns were fully loaded and in addition there were four five-inch rockets under each wing.

Preflight inspection complete, aircraft started and checked out. Then came the signal to launch aircraft. They taxied us on to the catapult for the "Cat Shot." We had asked the older pilots if there was any difference in flying these heavily loaded birds with the belly tanks - they said no "big" difference ......ha! After the Cat threw me off, I thought I was flying a heavy bomber, not a fighter. However, after gaining speed, with wheels and flaps up and trimmed up, she flew much better. Oh yes, had to remember to check and test my wing guns to make sure they were ready to perform. Then, off to the rendezvous.

We headed out on a Northwesterly heading as we were to rendezvous with the PBY at a point about 150 miles south of the main island of Kyushu, which was the southernmost island. The weather was good and we found the big bird without too much trouble. We carefully pulled abreast of her and then ahead so that they could positively identify us as friendly. This done, the PBY set course, with us flying high cover. We were pretty apprehensive over this flight because our strikes that morning had been against Kanoya airfield at the upper end of the bay. Felt sure they would scramble their fighters after us.

We arrived over the bay and the PBY dropped down to around 100-300 feet and started patrolling back and forth across the bay, trying to insure that every drop of water was looked at. The F4Us patrolled overhead around 10,000 feet, so we could intercept the enemy fighters. It is a mystery that they never showed up. Maybe our strike that morning hurt them more than we knew. Later, part of our flight dropped down to around 1000 feet to help the Cat (Catalina PBY) search. We were looking for a small raft in the water, dye marker, a very pistol signal flare or the reflections of a small hand held mirror. Still, we saw no signs.

The briefing officer had instructed us to be back before dark. Finally, our flight leader signaled the Dumbo that it was time for us to depart. After a few more passes, the Dumbo set course for the vicinity of Okinawa. We stayed with them for about 100 miles and then broke away and set course for the Task Group. We climbed to a higher altitude to pick up the Essex' navigational aid.

Pretty soon, we received a call from "Bobcat Base" (Essex) requesting our position. After that, CIC advised us to "buster" to home plate - maximum sustained speed as there were numerous "bogies" on the radar screen. Finally, they picked us up on radar and vectored us toward one of the bogies, who we felt sure was a "bandit" (enemy aircraft.) CIC directed us to go to max speed to intercept, but we still could not see them, even though they were reported to be only 2 to 4 miles ahead. Unfortunately, the sun had gone down and it was nearly dark. Finally the ship could wait no longer and ordered all aircraft to "stand clear salvo." This meant for all friendly aircraft to stand clear of the Task Group as they were opening all guns on the target. The flight leader quickly went into a steep bank and reversed course to clear the area. At a safe distance, we went into a lazy circle. I then saw a sight that is hard to describe. At that time, the entire Task Force of approximately 30 to 33 ships opened fire with all the AA guns they had. It was just like a city lighting up with all the flashes. Hard to believe that a plane could get through all that flack.

Our flight leader knew he had two greenhorns with him, so he called Bobcat Base and advised that he had two new "chicks" in his flight and requested that, if possible, they take us aboard right away before real dark-black dark set in. The reply was a short and terse "Negative." So we continued to circle with White and myself realizing that our first landing aboard Essex would be at night. Our training up until this point had included a few night approaches, but no landings.

Finally, the fleet signaled "all clear" and Bobcat Base signaled us "Charlie" - come in and land. Our flight leader found the ship and took us into the landing pattern. Besides being scared, I am sure I was jerky, over-controlling and fast as I groped my way along. My biggest problem was just finding the stern of the Essex. After finding it, then you sort of fly up the wake until you see the ship and hopefully some "weak" flight deck sut pan lights. The LSO (landing signal officer) worked hard and gave me every break, but still he had to waive me off on my first two approaches. By now it had been a long day as we had been in the cockpit for 4 and 1/4 hours. I started my 3rd approach, found the stern and the landing lights, continued up the groove and to my great relief and "fright," the LSO gave me a "cut" - signal to land. As many say, "any night landing that you can walk away from is a good one."

Frank Thigpen

14 April:

Ships Log-300 miles E. of Okinawa refueling and rearming

Wonder 21 (that's the call sign for our division-Coumbe, Wallace and me) is flying C A P (combat air patrol). The sky is clear. There is nothing in sight. I realize that today is my wife's birthday.

Thinking back to September 9th I recall flying from Ayer, Massachusetts to Pittsburgh, PA. I had called Mary Jayne and she had agreed to marry me three days prior. Flying?? LT (jg) Lynn Godson and I were flying an old SBD dive-bomber. This relic was on our base at Ayer.

The skipper said I could have 5 days off to go home and get married. Lynn had dated a Lt(jg) Marie Thompson when we were based at Atlantic City, NJ. Marie was in my high school class in Dormont, PA. Marie was home on leave at the time so it worked out quite well.

The SBD had two seats, one behind the other. I was flying from the front seat. As we approached the Greater Pittsburgh Airport, I called through the gossport (a tube connecting the two seats-used to talk to each other)." Lynn does it look clear to land.) I would have called the tower at the major airport for the city of Pittsburgh except the SBD did not have a radio. Lynn said" It looks ok to me" So I landed.

My daydreaming was interrupted by- Wonder21 this is wonder base. Do you read me?

F6F Hellcat

The F6F Hellcat had the highest Kill/Loss ratio of any American fighter plane in the Army, Navy, Marine or Air Force service during WWII. It was designed specifically to stop the Japanese Zero. (16 enemy planes shot down for each Hellcat lost)

During my tour of duty aboard the ESSEX our division usually flew a Corsair. However, when the Air Group Commander flew (not very often) we flew the Hellcat. I flew as his section leader. (We flew in groups of four, the division leader, his wingman and the section leader with his wingman)

The Hellcat was the real workhorse of the carrier fleet. The Corsair was faster. However I would choose the Hellcat if we were in an old fashioned dogfight. It was more maneuverable and could take a lot of punishment.

We were in a number of dogfights at the beginning of our tour. Later we learned to gain height advantage, make a pass and pull up for another pass rather than stay in the melee.

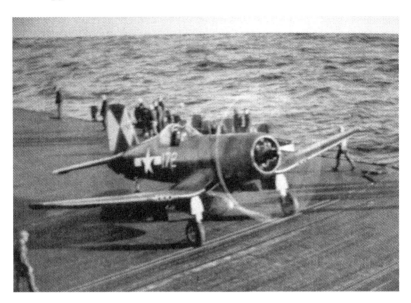

The split diamonds on the tail was used while we were aboard ship. We thought the Japanese had pieced together workable planes from crashes. Each carrier had different identification markings on the tail and wing sections. If you attempted to land on a ship other than your own, you would be shot down.

F6F-3 "Hellcats in Flight," 1943
National Museum of Naval Aviation

Photo: National Archives and Records Administration
There were many heroic men who served on the deck crew.

If we did not drop our bomb, we brought it back to the ship. Upon landing a 500-pound bomb came loose from a Hellcat as the forward progress was violently stopped when the plane caught a wire. Three men of the deck crew ran out and pushed the bomb to the edge of the ship. I don't know where they got the strength as they picked the bomb up and tossed it clear of the gunnery station that stuck out beyond the deck.

V F

O F F I C E R S

ANDERSON, Kenneth J., Ens.	Eau Claire, Wis.
BATTEN, Hugh N., Lt. (jg)	Huntington, W. Va.
BEAUMONT, James, Lt. (jg)	Pittsburgh, Pa.
BEEMER, Eldon C., Ens.	Carlton, Kansas
BLANTON, Beatty S., Lt. Comdr.	Charlotte, N. C.
BOUTWELL, Emmett B., Lt. (jg)	Covington, Ky.
BREWER, Robert H., Ens.	Cincinnati, Ohio
BROCATO, Samuel J., Lt. (jg)	Baltimore, Md.
CASEY, Eugene G., Ens.	Granite City, Ill.
CLARK, Clyde S., Ens.	Amarillo, Texas
CLARK, Lawrence A., Lt. (jg)	Bell, Calif.
CLARK, Rosser L., Jr., Lt. (jg)	Greensboro, N. C.
COLEMAN, Thaddeus T., Jr., Lieut.	Eastman, Ga.
COLVIN, Louis E., Ens.	Seattle, Wash.
COMMELLA, Samual E., Lt. (jg)	New Brighton, Pa.
CONDOR, Thomas L., Jr., Lieut.	Decatur, Ga.
CRITES, Simon, Jr., Lt. (jg)	Corpus Christi, Texas
CROWTHER, Thomas B., Lt. (jg)	Greystone, R. I.
DAVIDSON, Paul D., Lt. (jg)	North Platte, Nebr.
DAVIS, Edwin B., Lt. (jg)	Chattanooga, Tenn.
ELY, John C., Lieut.	Glasgow, Ky.
EMERLING, Raymond J., Jr., Lt. (jg)	Hamburg, N. Y.
ESTES, Willian E., Lt. (jg)	Bronxville, N. Y.
FALLWELL, Beeman N., Lt. (jg)	Raleigh, N. C.
FARRELL, James J., Lt. (jg)	Staten Is., N. Y.
GARRARD, Robert B., Lieut.	Greenwood, Miss.
HAMILTON, Robert M., Lt. (jg)	Baldwin, L. I., N. Y.
HERTIG, William S., Lt. (jg)	Quincy, Ill.
HANNAWAY, Robert F., Lt. (jg)	Columbus, Ohio
HUBENTHAL, Charles E., Lt. (jg)	Lucerne, Indiana
KINGSTON, William J., Jr., Ens.	Jersey City, N. J.
KOLBE, Myron E., Lt. (jg)	Wellington, Ohio
LA METTRY, Robert, Ens.	Minneapolis, Minn.
LANGDON, Richard H., Ens.	Moorestown, N. J.

LARKIN, John R., Jr., Lt. (jg)	Baltimore, Md.
LETTO, Thomas "L", Jr., Lieut.	Orange, Calif.
LOWE, Max F., Jr., Lt. (jg)	Daytona Beach, Fla.
LYNCH, John M., Lt. (jg)	Boston, Mass.
LYONS, Jack M., Lt. (jg)	Long Beach, Calif.
MAKI, Jack M., Lt. (jg)	Conneaut, Ohio
McCARTY, Loren J., Ens.	St. Cloud, Minn.
McMASTER, Alvin R., Ens.	Richmond, Calif.
McPHERSON, Donald M., Ens.	Adams, Nebraska
MEATTE, Luke L., Ens.	Portageville, Mo.
MINAR, George, Lt. (jg)	Kenosha, Wis.
MOHR, Max D., Lieut.	St. Paul, Minn.
MORTON, William J., Ens.	Salisbury, N. C.
ROBERTSON, Lorell W. A., Lt. (jg)	Tulsa, Okla.
ROBINSON, David., Lt. Comdr.	Perth Amboy, N. J.
ROTH, Owen R., Ens.	Rochester, N. Y.
SAMPSON, Willard A., Lt. Comdr.	Evanston, Ill.
SCHAUB, Gerald R., Lt. (jg)	Glenwood, Minn.
SOFFE, Carlos R., Lieut.	Midvale, Utah
STURDIVANT, Archibald Y., Jr., Lieut.	Minter City, Mississippi
SULLIVAN, Rex "E", Jr., Ens.	Quanah, Texas
THOMS, Joseph I., Ens.	Huntington, W. Va.
TIPTON, Billie, Lt. (jg)	Caruthersville, Missouri
TITUS, John K., Lt. (jg)	Woodstown, N. J.
TRUAX, Myron M., Ens.	Ft. Worth, Texas
UMPHFRES, Donald E., Lieut.	Phillips, Texas
WALDOCH, Daniel V., Lt. (jg)	Forest Lake, Minn.
WARD, Lyttleton T., Lt. (jg)	Norfolk, Va.
WARRIOR, Joseph D., Ens.	Independence, Mo.
WEAVER, David F., Lieut.	Kansas City, Mo.
WHITTAKER, Donald L. A., Lt. (jg)	Quincy, Mass.
WIESNER, Raymond A., Ens.	Manitowoc, Wis.
WILSON, Billie L., Lt. (jg)	E. Akron, Ohio

VF ENLISTED MEN

BLUE, Durward M., ACRM	Orlando, Fla.
BREWER, Harold K., ARTlc	Lavaca, Ark.
BUCHANAN, George F., AMMlc	Washington, D.C.
BUGBEE, Edward H. II, AMM2c	Williamsport, Pa.
CATCHINGS, Clifford D., ACOM	Columbus, Ga.
DEETJEN, Donald A., Ylc	Chicago, Ill.
DRAPER, Douglas, AOMlc	Sacramento, Cal.
GENCARELLE, Salvatore A., AOMlc	Westerly, R. I.
GERKEN, Henry L., AMMlc	Santa Ana, Cal.
HAFT, Jacob G., Jr., ARTlc	Cincinnati, Ohio
HORVATH, John J., ACMM	Dover, N. J.
McKIBBEN, Jack B., AEMlc	San Jacinto, Cal.

MURPHY, Robert J., Jr., AMM2c	Chillicothe, Mo.
O'NEILL, Eugene D., PhoM2c	Cottage City, Md.
OWINGS, Oscar B., AMM1c	Memphis, Tenn.
PAPADOPOULOS, John, PR1c	Washington, D. C.
PARKER, Carl L., ARM3c	Ashville, N. C.
PATTON, David A., AMM1c	Philadelphia, Pa.
POPE, John M., ART1c	Arnold, Nebr.
POSCH, Richard T., ART1c	Chicago, Ill.
SKELLEN, Earle C., AEM1c	Kent, N. Y.
SMITH, David L., ACM1c	Saylesville, R. I.
WIGHAMAN, John C., AMM1c	Lima, Ohio
YOUNG, Joseph W., AM1c	Rushville, Ind.

16 April:

During a sweep over Kyushu we lost Bouldin, Wear and Tommy Ward. Wear and Ward went into the water and a rescue mission (with Thigpen and White) is looking for them.

Ham Reidy saw Bouldin on the ground beside his plane. Assume he became a POW, as we never heard from him again. (This includes after the war)

Fleet under attack all day. Kamikazes hit 8 ships, 2 Destroyers were sunk. The Intrepid was hit again. Tommy Ward was picked up by a PBY but Wear could not be found.

I {(Lt jg) Pappert} was asked to gather Boldin's belongings so they could be shipped back to the states. In his locker was a shopping bag with 18 clocks. The mystery of the clocks missing from the F4Us has been solved. Or had it? This would have been an ideal way for the clock thief to dispose of his loot. The clocks were given to the maintenance crew. They were not reported as part of Bouldin's belongings.

17 April:

Fleet under attack most of the day. AA splashed 3 Kamikazes diving on our ship. Clem Wear was picked up. Two Intrepid pilots shot down a B25. The Intrepid is going home.

18 April:

Today we have been in combat one month. One SB2C (dive bomber) spun in on landing. Pilot not recovered. Lt "Rock" (reportedly an all American tackle from USC) was killed on take off due to a faulty catapult shot.

19-22 April:

Air group flew numerous missions over Okinawa in support of the big push by our ground troops. 5 Japs shot down near the fleet. Last transmission of one of them was "Banzi". Lt. Kinkade made the 25,000 landing aboard the Essex. (Air Group 83 made over 3,000 landings in the past 30 days.)

23-27 April:

Lots of bombing and straffing on Okinawa and outlying islands. "The Greek" shot a horse. Two SB2Cs had a mid air collision.

We were flying cover for the SB2Cs (dive bombers) on a mission over Okinawa. On the way back we saw one SB2C fly into the tail of another. One of the planes turned over. The other was flying erratically. The air was full of pilots yelling, "Bail out". Then we saw 4 parachutes open. However they opened just before the airmen hit the drink. We were only about 2,000 feet above the sea when this happened. The pilots and crewmen were rescued.

The Helldive-designated as SB2C

In identification circles, it was called Son of a Bitch Second Class (SB2C) Much has been written about the Helldiver. Most of it, said it was a lousy plane. It was the last plane built by Curtis Wright that was accepted by the Navy.

It may have been a hard plane to fly and a disappointment to the Navy, but the pilots of Air Group 83 had a great record.

Summary of Damage To The Enemy
By Bombing 83

Ships sunk and ground targets destroyed includes some sinkings or
destruction in coordination with other aircraft.

	Damaged	Sunk
Carriers	2	
Battleships	3	1
Cruisers	2	
Submarines		2
Torpedo Boats		2
Honshu-Hokkaido Ferries		3
Merchant Ships	4	8
Total Tonnage	185,000tons	60,000 tons

Ground Targets	Damaged	Destroyed
Aircraft	12	3
Hangers	13	9
Barracks	9	6
Warehouses	10	6
Lighthouses	1	
Dry-docks	1	
Bridges	7	2
Fuel Tanks		6
Ferry Slips	5	
Railroads	5	
Ammunition Dumps		4
Submarine Pens	6	7
Pillboxes	5	2
Anti-aircraft Batteries	1	7
Artillery Emplacements	6	
Tanks		1

V B

O F F I C E R S

BLAIR, Robert H., Ens.	Berryville, Va.
BREECE, David K., Ens.	Albuquerque, N. M.
BRESLOVE, Joseph, Jr., Lieut.	Pittsburgh, Pa.
CARLSON, Nils A. A., Lt. (jg)	Salt Lake City, Utah
CHADWICK, Kenneth F., Lt. (jg)	Chattanooga, Tenn.
CRAWFORD, James T., Lieut.	Memphis, Tenn.
ELLIS, Kermit Q., Lt. (jg)	Lexington, Mo.
ESHERICK, Joseph, Jr., Lt. (jg)	Ross, California
GOODRICH, Robert R., Lieut.	Fort Worth, Texas
GORDON Leo, Lt. (jg)	N. Hollywood, Calif.
GORHAM, William W., Lt. (jg)	Glendale, Calif.
HUTTO, Ernest E., Ens.	Decatur, Ala.
MARSHALL, Walton H., Jr., Lieut.	Orange, Virginia
MITCHELL, Shelby W., Lieut.	Wesson, Mississippi

MONAGHAN, James E., Ens.   Ely, Nevada

OLNEY, Sheldon, Lieut.   Canyon, Calif.

PLOG, Leonard H., Ens.   Hood River, Oregon

PYNE, Insley B., Lieut.   Far Hills, New Jersey

RINER, James A., Jr., Lieut.   Chicago 4, Illinois

ROSS, Guilford N., Lieut.   Pleasant Garden, N. C.

ROYSTER, Charles F., Jr., Ens.   Catlin, Ill.

STANLAKE, Joseph D., Ens.   Duluth, Minn.

THOMPSON, Berkeley S., Lieut.   Delhi, N. Y.

TOLFORD, Jack J., Lt. (jg)   Toledo, Ohio

WATKINS, Edward L., Lt. (jg)   Springfield, Mo.

WEEKS, Elbert C., Lt. (jg)   Natchitoches, La.

WELLEN, William H., Lt. (jg)   Marlboro, Mass.

E N L I S T E D   M E N

ALLEN, Daniel F., ARM1c	Winchester, N. H.
AVERA, William D., ARM3c	Fort Valley, Ga.
BOSLER, Judson H., AMM2c	Rensselaer, N. Y.
BROPHY, Joseph F., ARM2c	Quincy, Mass.
BROWN, Gardner N., ACRM	Edgartown, Mass.
BROWN, Joe, Jr., ARM2c	Shelby, N. C.
BRULAND, Theodore W., AOM1c	Brooklyn, N. Y.
CADDEN, James M., AMM2c	Victoria, Texas
CADIEUX, Harold F., ARM2c	Milford, Conn.
CAMPBELL, Walter R. H., ARM1c	Amsterdam, N. Y.
CAPPIELLO, Michael A., Jr., ARM2c	Bridgeport, Conn.
COOPER, Robert F., ARM3c	Rector, Arkansas
CROSS, Clifford C., ARM3c	Scappoose, Oregon
DURFEE, Winthrop C., Y1c	Hartford, Conn.
ERKENBRACK, Donald J., ARM1c	Superior, Wis.
GIGANTE, Arthur F., AMM2c	Brooklyn, N. Y.
HILDEBRAND, Leslie D., AEM1c	Marble Rock, Iowa
HUBNER, Joseph G., ARM3c	Rochester, N. Y.
JURAVCOFF, Dimitri P., AMM1c	San Francisco, Calif.
KELLEY, George R., ARM2c	Chevy Chase, Md.

LAVINE, Edward V., ARM3c	Pittsburgh, Pa.
LEVINE, Manny, ARM3c	Hillside, N. J.
LOVAS, James F., ARM3c	Peterson, N. J.
MACKINAC, Frank G., ARTlc	Chicago, Ill.
MITCHELL, Robert L., ACOM	Augusta, Ga.
PALERMO, Sullivan A., ARM3c	East Patchogue, L. I., N. Y.
POTTER, Sam G., ARM3c	Condon, Oregon
QUIRK, Vincent P., ARM2c	South Boston, Mass.
REYNOLDS, James A., ARM3c	Patchogue, N. Y.
RICE, Aaron A., ARM3c	Anderson, S. C.
ROCHAT, Charles A., Jr., AMlc	Sea Cliff, N. Y.
SCHAEFFER, William J., ARM3c	Reading, Pa.
SHANER, Ralph E., AMMlc	Ellwood City, Pa.
SHAY, Richard L., ARMlc	Springfield, Ohio
STERNER, William W., ARM2c	Reading, Pa.
STRICKLAND, Dellie B., ACMM	Baltimore, Md.
SULLIVAN, Harry J., ARM2c	Pittsburgh, Pa.
WAGNER, John W., ARMlc	New York 18, N. Y.
WEBBER, John F., Prlc	Compton, Calif.

28 April/2 May:

Wallace on Okinawa

32 Jap planes shot down over Okinawa. Heard garbled word on German surrender. One of our hospital ships was bombed by Japs-167 killed and 17 wounded. Weather very bad.

4 May:

Good weather. Everything launched. The air group shot down 38 Japs today. Lost Gibby from the squadron. One of our Destroyers was sunk and two more damaged by kamikazes 207 Jap planes downed by us since 18 March (46 days). The task force has destroyed over 1,000 enemy planes since 1 April (34 days).

7 May:

Flew Shipping strike at Amimi - dropped 1000 pound bomb and strafed ships in harbor. Dropped incendiaries on Kikai. Quite a bit of AA up there and bad weather don't help.. A Corsair cracked up on flight deck. Pilot hurt.

8 MAY:

Bad weather.. sea getting rough. Heard war is over in Europe. Doesn'tseem to mean much out here. Bet everyone back home is getting pie eyed.. Rumor has it we will go to Leyete last of this month to provisions.

9 MAY:

We have been making gadgets in our room. Lost two very good friends today. Smitty was shot down by AA over Amami. Jimmy Tucker was killed last night when taking off from the Enterprise which is cruising right behind us.. The Skipper came in and brought some "Medicinal Brandy". Didn't leave until 0300. Pappert, Coumbe and I feeling no pain.

10 MAY:

Refueled.

11 MAY:

Flew Close Air Support for Marine troops on Okinawa. My plane shot up by ground fire and made dead stick landing at Yonton field,

13 MAY:

Slept on the ground and ate K rations. Had a bombing raid by Japs. Checked on getting my plane fixed. Saw all the boys from the Bunker Hill. They were going back to the states.

14 MAY:

Went up in the hills of North Okinawa. Saw lots of Natives and burned out stuff. I also checked out some caves. Heard later they were Jap Soldiers in the caves.. Jap planes raided us about dark. Our AA got one but a Suicide plane hit a Battleship in the harbor… Found a cot in a Marine tent to sleep on. Dust very bad.

15 MAY:

Went up to the front lines. Saw lots of dead Marines and Japs. The stink was awful.. Bulldozers were covering up the Japs. Had another bombing raid about 0200. Spent most of the night in a Foxhole.

I wore my flight suit all the time on the ground. It got quite smelly, but so did the Marines so nobody noticed. I left word with the tower to get in touch with me if they saw any Essex planes come in. Then I went sight seeing Found a cave full of drums of Japanese gasoline. I came back and proudly reported same to the Marines in our tent. They scoffed and explained that it was of such low octane it would not burn in our jeeps. However, they did show me how to cook with it by filling a can with rocks, pouring the gas in and lighting it. I also found one cave with stacks of ammo boxes. Brought back a case and again the Marines were ahead of me. The cases were full of coned shaped brass, coned shaped brass fuses for Jap AA guns. I was shown how to unscrew them and burn off the black powder. They could be used as a paperweight. I brought a few back to the ship.

I was a very junior officer and on my first experience with a night bombing raid by Japs. I almost became a dead junior officer. The night sky was ablaze with searchlights, tracer fire and bomb explosions. To me it was an exciting fireworks display. I stood and gawked until one of the Marines helped me into a fox hole with his big boondocker boots.

The white woman referred to was a Navy Nurse here to evacuate the wonded. She was a blond wearing a skin tight nylon Navy flight suit. Everything came to a halt while she was there and for some reason many, many Marines found a reason to be in the vicinity.

After I joined up with two Essex planes, it was discovered that I could not raise them on the radio as I did not know the frequency they were using. Neither did I know the identification call of the day for the ship. I just tucked in close and flew wing on them till we arrived in the vicinity of the ship and got the usual burst of AA from them. This was not uncommon because everybody on board was so stressed out and trigger happy. They would shoot first and ask questions later.

Landed aboard a very clean ship with very clean aircraft with my muddy plane and dirty flight suit. It sure stood out.

16 MAY:

It rained all night. No raid by Japs. Saw a white woman (Nurse). Mud knee deep. Saw two planes from the Essex come in. Jumped in a plane and joined up with them. Flew back to the ship.. Found out the Enterprise had a bad hit by a Kamikaze and is going home. So is our Skipper.

17 MAY:

Flew patrol over Amami - dropped fire bombs, Strafed and fired rockets on boats and AA guns. set a plane on fire on the ground.. AA getting much worse up there.

18 MAY:

Flew 0500 CAP at 25000 feet, Made strike on Amami. We lost two torpedo planes. My good friend Boatright, was flying one of them. Rest of the month will be same-o-same according to flight schedule.

19 May:

We flew close air support over Okinawa. Many of our planes hit by ground fire (including mine). Essex under attack. Splashed a couple of Kamikazes. Bunker Hill hit by two Kamikazes and is badly damaged. The Enterprise hit again and is going home.

We were standing on the bridge when a Kamikaze flew across our ship and exploded on the Bunker Hill. The Bunker Hill was our sister ship. That is she cruised about 1,000 yards to our left and kept pace with us. With this Vern, Glen and I made a hasty retreat to our room. The loud speaker was on. Our Chaplin came on and said" There are three enemy planes approaching the fleet. They are about half mile away. They are in their dive. One is bearing down on us. Take cover. It's ok, our gunners got him." He splashed within 100 yards of the ship. The Chaplin was quite a guy. He kept a running account of all enemy planes as they approached the fleet.

19-23 May:

Flew strikes in bad weather. Ens. Jones spun in. He was buried at sea this evening. Japs attacked the ships around Okinawa with 35 planes and several submarines We shot down 25 of the planes and sank some of the subs, plus two Jap destroyers and one transport. Some of our ships were damaged. Tomorrow we go Jap hunting.

24-27 May:

50-plane sweep on Kyushu, Japan. Rockets and bombs for everything on the ground. Two Zekes splashed. Two Pelican Planes went down. Flew Combat Air Patrol in very bad weather, 200 ft. ceiling and quarter mile visibility. Big Jap attack on Okinawa. Some landed and destroyed several of our planes on the ground.

28 May:

Pre-dawn launch. Three Jap planes splashed. One of our planes downed by a Tony. The task force has been changed from Task Force 58 to Task Force 38. McCane and Halsey replaced Mitchner and Spruance.

I received a letter about two weeks later. My wife (Mary Jayne) was delighted. She said the newspaper reported that Task Force 58 replaced Task Force 38. She knew I was coming home. –They replaced the top brass-everything else remained the same. Sorry Mary Jayne, the pilots are still fighting.

29 May:

No fly. We are on our way to Leyte (Philippine Islands) after 79 days at sea. We all got Cholera shots and saw our first movie-a stinker.

It was reported that we were at sea longer than any other fighting force. As mentioned before our food was for the most part good. However, the flour got infected with bugs. A chemical was added to kill the bugs. This resulted in the bread taking on a light purple color. So, we held the bread up to the light and picked out the small black spots (bugs). The bread toasted just fine.

1 June:

Dropped the anchor at 0927. We have steamed over 33,000 miles in 2 ½ months and flew over 25,000flight hours.

2-18 June:

Tacloban Beach. Everybody really getting limbered up. A P-38 crashed into the Randolph a few hundred yards from us. (He was showing off. Killed some people and bashed a bunch of planes on deck.) The Hornet and Bennington arrived after coming through a Typhoon. They are really beat up. Probably state side jobs. Air Groups 9,12,17,and 82 going home. We are now the Senior Air Group.

Nothing much happened during our rest stop in the Philippines. We drank beer and swam in the ocean. That was a mistake. I got an inner ear infection from swimming. That put me in Sickbay. Purple liquid was poured into the ear for about a week. Then orders called for the Essex to go back into action. At that time I was given a shot glass full of sulfa pills and told to take them all at one time. This cleared up the problem. Well, I can still whistle through the ear if I try. I do not try very often.

We did walk into town while we were on the beach. The town consisted of a few huts. The market was an open air one. Fish (about three feet long) were dried and stacked like cordwood. A youngster was carrying a piece of meat. It was not wrapped. A string was tied to the meat. He held the string. The meat dangled about two inches from the ground. The vegetation was unbelievable. Plants had leaves four feet long. This was understandable as the temperature was in the nineties and you could set you watch by the consistence of the rain, that came everyday at about two P M.

27 April:

The Greek shoots a horse

One of our good friends was and is known as "The Greek" His name is Jim Sakes.

The Greek wrote the following:

In April of 1945, Bill Wood's division consisted of Bill Wood, myself as his wingman, Pat Flanders and Fred Strause. We were flying Combat Air Patrol at around 10,000 feet over Okinawa.

Bill Wood noticed a moving object on a highway and put us into a right upper echelon. We pealed off to attack the moving object. Bill overshot the target and I managed to hit it. When we got back to the Essex, I was credited with shooting a horse.

On April 7,1945 Bill Woods division was in condition 10 status (ready to take off) when the U.S.S. Hancock's flight deck which was loaded with aircraft ready to be launched, was wiped out by a Kamikaze. The Essex had to turn to match the turns of the Hancock and could not get into the wind to launch our aircraft.

We were finally launched and vectored to intercept a flight of Judies. I was credited with splashing one of the Judies. Shortly thereafter I started experiencing engine trouble, but could not land on the Essex because she was spotted aft for the next launch. I landed on the aircraft carrier Bataan. I had gone through flight training with many of the junior officers and was known to them as "The Greek".

I was the guest of honor and dined at the Captain's table. Three days later while on a search mission, I again experienced engine trouble and had to land on the Bataan. The engine died while still in the arresting gear. As I was climbing out of the cockpit, the air boss (using his air horn) said "Welcome home Greek. Next time bring your damned mess share.

6th of May: Sam Takes a Wave Off:

Vern and I are standing on the bridge watching landings. The F6F squadron is just returning. It's late in the afternoon. The last two planes are coming in. They seem to be about right. The next-to-the-last F6F catches a wire, but the crew is a little slower than normal in getting it released, so the Landing Signal Officer gives the pilot a wave-off.

Normally when a pilot gets a wave-off, he flies parallel to the ship for a mile or two, makes two left-hand turns, comes back past the ship, makes two more left-hand turns, comes in, and lands.

In this case, this F6F, when he got the wave-off, immediately put the plane in a hard left-hand turn, and made a 360-degree circle just beside the ship, and in no time at all was right back at the tail end of the ship and in position. He got a cut and he landed. When he pulled forward, the loudspeaker came on, and the Captain said, "This is the Captain. Will the pilot of the plane that just landed report to the bridge." The pilot who had just landed was Sam Brocato. The captain gave him a real chewing-out for making the landing that he had.

Actually, we all thought it was a great piece of flying, but as the Captain explained, only a real experienced, expert pilot could get away with that. He had to know his ship well enough to know he was completely airborne and wouldn't fall out of the sky. The danger there would be not having enough power, and being too slow the plane could crash. The skipper explained to him that most of the pilots were not able to do what Sam did and they might attempt to do it. The skipper then over the loudspeaker said, "No one will ever do this again. When you take a wave-off you fly forward for a mile, then make two left-hand turns and make your normal approach."

Flashback: Sam Brocato was one of my very good friends. He went through training at Jacksonville, FL along with Jack Ely, Huey Batten, Jim Farrell and Sully (Joseph Sullivan). We had just been commissioned prior to that, except for Jack Ely, he was a "jg, he joined us there. This was operational training.

Operational training meant that we were flying heavier aircraft and learning formation flying. In this case we were flying the F4F, (the Wildcat) that was used in the beginning of the war. It was a good little airplane, but not fast enough to compete with the Japanese Zeros. However, it was our training plane. The six of us were based at Jacksonville, Florida. I remember we did have Thanksgiving dinner at the base one day. I think it was the only meal we ate at the base. Our routine at the end of the day was to go to town, have dinner, stay in town for the night, and return the next morning. One day we did this, immediately returning to the flight line. We were a little bit late and we were having gunnery practice.

Gunnery practice means that one of us had to tow a sleeve. The sleeve was a wire mesh about four or five feet across and probably thirty feet long. A long cable was attached to the plane and the cable was stretched out along with the mesh target in front of you. You revved up the plane and got going as fast as you could, and pulled up into the air. This took quite a jerk as the drag of the wire and the cable was pretty much a strain for the F4F. Anyway, one of us would tow the target out over the ocean and the others would then make runs at it, that is, they would be above the target plane, they'd make a run down and shoot at the target. The bullets of each of the planes were colored with paint so that when you were done and you came back and they released the target, they could count how many hits you had made. Well, we did this. However, you would never have enough ammunition. There was an outlying field where we would stop and re-arm. This we did. I happened to be towing the target that day. When I came back in, I said, "Where's Sam?" They said, "Oh, Sam was scheduled to report to the sick bay." I said, "What happened?" They said, "Well, when he landed he ground-looped." Now ground-looping an F4F is no criticism of any pilot. The landing gear on the F4F is about three feet across. It's like landing on a rudder, and the wings could dip down and ground-loop, or at least dip down and scrape on the ground. If you have a ground loop, you must report and have a doctor check you. When Sam went in to be checked, he took

off his flight suit. Of course he still had on his white shirt and his Navy blue pants, as we were in town the night before in dress. The doc looked at him and said, "Son, tell me this. Are you getting ready to go, or are you just coming back?" We thought it was rather amusing.

Speaking of ground-looping a plane, while we were at Jacksonville I was coming for a landing on a landing strip that paralleled the hangars. Now the hangars, around them, had small grass areas and the grass areas were roped off with clothesline. The purpose of this was to keep all sailors and all personnel from walking across the lawn. When I came in and landed the plane, the left wing dropped, and over the radio I could hear "field closed." The left wing dropped, it didn't hit the ground, but it clipped the clotheslines of about four or five of those grassed areas, just clipped them right off and broke them. After the plane lost air speed, the plane righted itself and came back on its two wheels. Next thing over the radio, I heard "field open." I taxied around and parked the plane, no problem, and no report as no damage was done to the airplane.

Ed Pappert   Sam Brocato   Jim Farrell
        Jack Ely   Hugh Batten   Joe Sullivan

Ed Pappert-Author

Jack Ely-A Physician living in Spokane, Washington

Sam Brocato- Stayed in the service. Killed in a mid air collision in Japan

Hugh Batten- Retired as a Captain USN-Died of a heart attack

Jim Farrell-Went to Syracuse-became a lawyer Whereabouts unknown

Joe Sullivan-Was a landing signal officer-Has not kept in touch.

In the picture the third fellow to my left is Huey Batten. As I said, Huey was probably the best pilot I ever knew. He stayed in the service and retired as a Captain. He became a test pilot and trained with most of the original astronauts. As I understand it, Huey could have been an astronaut except that he did not have a college education. They offered to send him to school and get the education, but he refused.

When we were in Massachusetts, we took a few hops back to our homes towns. Huey was from somewhere in West Virginia, I believe it was Huntington, West Virginia. When Huey came back, he was called in by the squadron commander (Pug Southerland) and told that there was a report in that he had been seen flying very low over a swimming pool in his home town. They said some Army officer has gotten his wing number and said he was flying just over the flagpole. Huey said, "I know that's wrong, I had to look up at that flagpole." Anyway, Huey was put in hack for a week. "In hack" means that he had to stay in his room, with supposedly a Marine guard outside to keep him there.

While we were in the waiting room at Ayer, Massachusetts, the skipper, Pug Sutherland, overheard Huey asking Sam to loan him twenty bucks until next payday. The skipper said, "Tell me something, why would you need money? You're getting pay as an Ensign, and flight pay. You have a place to live, your food's provided. What do you do with your money?" Huey thought for a minute, and he said, "Well, about 80 percent goes for whiskey and women, and I just waste the other 20 percent."

To my immediate left is Jack Ely. He and I roomed together while we were based at Atlantic City. He would drive his car on the Boardwalk. It was against the law of course. One night when the police were blowing their whistles at us, he turned to leave the Boardwalk. Instead of a street, he turned into the entrance of a hotel. Upon backing up, the car ran into a cement lamp post. He then drove down a ramp onto Atlantic avenue. Unfortunately one of the fenders was rubbing against a tire. Another policeman got his license number.

The police tracked the license plates. In court, Jack said he was at the Officers' club the night of the accident. The prosecuting attorney asked how Jack could explain the damage to his fender and the fact that the police had his license number. Jack's story was that he left the keys in the car as several of the wives of our squadron mates were pregnant and they had his permission to use his car if needed. He got off with a fine for the cost of replacing the lamppost. He could lie better than I could tell the truth.

Next to Jack is Sam Brocato. Sam and Hughie Batten (next to Sam) were two of my best friends. Hughie Batten was probably the best pilot in our squadron. Sam was just about as good. On one mission they separated from the group. They were flying Hellcats. Six Japanese Zeros jumped them. Sam and Hughie shot down all six of them. They had the cameras on so all kills were confirmed.

Next is Jim Farrell. Jim lived on Staten Island. I stayed at his house for four days. He had a good-looking sister. Best I not go further on this. Toward the end of our tour, Jim left the squadron. They said it was combat fatigue. After the war ended, Jim went to Syracuse. He became a lawyer.

The last pilot in the photo was Sullivan. After this picture was taken, Sullivan crashed in the St. Johns River. He got out unhurt. His flying days were over. He became a landing signal officer.

June 1945 R & R in the Philippine Islands.

Lt(jg)s Glen Wallace, Ed Pappert, Vern Coumbe and Lynn Godson

June, 1945:

Our friend Jimmy the Greek writes:

While drinking beer at Macarata Beach on the island of Samara, while anchored in Leyte Gulf, I struck up a conversation with the captain of an LST and 6 Army nurses. The nurses were stationed at an army hospital at Tacloban. They indicated that they had been on LSTs, Destroyers and Cruisers but never on a carrier.

I of course invited them to be my guest and we took of in the LST for the Essex. The ships crew had not seen a woman in 19 months and almost rioted. Of course they were gentlemen and made them feel welcome. Preparatory to having them as our guests in the Officer's Wardroom, I cleared out the Junior Officer's head aft of the Junior Officer's bunkroom so they could primp themselves up. We all had a wonderful time at dinner. We bade them farewell and good luck as they embarked for Tacloban. The next day an occupant of the bunkroom said "I know I had a lot to drink yesterday but I could have sworn I heard woman's voices in the head"

Meanwhile, Glen, Vern, Lynn Godson and I (Ed Pappert) drank beer on the island and never saw any of this.

4 July:

Headed for Tokyo. We lost two pilots. The Aircraft Carrier Ticonderoga left the fleet. She is headed for Pearl Harbor.

Its 11 P. M. the four of us, Vern Coumbe, Glen Wallace, Clem Wear and I are playing Acey Deucy. Clem says "What were you doing last Fourth of July". Glen answers "I think that was about the time our division flew to the Grumman plant on Long Island." As I remember—

Flashbacks:

We are at Ayer, Massachusetts. We've just formed the squadron, and began our training in combat tactics. However, in July we were getting some leeway to take some cross-country hops for the experience.

I don't know how it came about, but our division, this was James Stevens, Vern Coumbe, Glen Wallace and I, were asked to fly to a Grumman factory in Bethpage, Long Island. We were told that we were to wear our best dress-blue uniforms, which we did.

When we got to Bethpage, L.I., the factory was there, and had one runway. We all landed with no problems, got out. Then we were asked to go through the plant as sort of a morale builder for the people working in the plant. I guess most of them were women at that time. We did, and along the way we stopped and made a few comments and told them about flying the Hellcat (which we were flying at that time). We told them what a great airplane we thought it was and how appreciative we were of their building it for us.

Along about four o'clock we decided we had better get back to Ayer, Massachusetts, so we took off. As we were flying back the weather closed in, I mean it really closed in. There was no way we could fly back through the weather. Stevens looked around and we were near Providence, Rhode Island. So we landed at the airport, took a cab into town and got a hotel room. We thought, "Boy, what a good time we're going to have here." Four Navy pilots in Providence, Rhode Island, I think it was a Saturday night and so far as we knew there were no Army or Navy installations nearby – or if there were, there weren't many, so we thought we would have a great time.

However, we'd been up very early, and had of course gotten pretty tired. There was no shower so I decided to take a bath. While I was in the bathtub I fell asleep, at that time James our leader decided the four of us had better call it a night and just rest up, which we did.

The next morning we got up, had breakfast and got a cab to the airport. About two-thirds of the way to the airport we got into a traffic jam and thought, gee, this was kind of unusual for a Sunday morning, why would there be a traffic jam?

We asked the cab driver, "what's going on?" He said, "Oh, haven't you heard – four Navy planes landed at the airport last night, and everybody in town is going out to see them." We said, "well, don't worry about the crowd, they won't take off before we get there." When we got there the control tower asked us if we would put on an air show as the townspeople had come out to see us. Would we buzz the tower? We told them we'd like to, BUT every time one of us did something like that some eager beaver Army officer, or Navy officer, would get our numbers and turn us in, and we would be in for at least a week in hack. He said, "I'll tell you what, when you get airborne I'll call you and tell you I don't think your wheels retracted properly. Will you fly close by the hangars so that I can check it out? That way if anybody reports it I'll have a record here that I asked you to do this."

That's all we needed. So to put on an air show, we took off in formation. This is kind of unusual because I don't think the Army ever lets their pilots take off in formation. When we got in the air the control tower called us and said, "I don't think your wheels retracted, would you mind flying close by the observation deck so we can check it." We all took turns buzzing the air traffic control. After we did that, we flew up a couple thousand feet in the air and did a few aerobatics – couple of loops, slow rolls, snaps – no we didn't do a snap, not in a fighter plane, that would have been disastrous. But we put on a little air show for them, then we said goodbye and flew back to Ayer, Massachusetts.

Two days later we received a package from the Grumman Aircraft Company. It was a rolled-up paper and inside it were watercolors, one of the F6F in flight and one of the F4F in flight. They were beautiful watercolors. I sent them home and my mother had them framed. Right now they're hanging in my son's garage.

2nd Flashback:

While we were in Ayer, Massachusetts we were using an Army field that was next to Fort Devens Hospital. Fort Devens is a large Army hospital that treated wounded brought back from the European theater. We used the airstrip, which was adjacent to the hospital. The accommodations, though, were not what we normally had. As Naval officers we always had nice rooms and were treated quite well.

Here there was a large barracks that reminded us of when we were cadets with big bunks lined up in rows. Well, we didn't particularly care for this, so we all looked over the area and in groups of four, we found cabins that were on lakes, to rent.

Four of us rented a cabin. There was Jack Ely, Lyn Godson, myself and Jim Bouldin. Anyway, it was about thirty-five or forty miles west of the city of Boston. There were no military installations in the area; there was one nightclub, or roadhouse, in the area. We called it "The Snake Pit." As there were no military installations around, all the young girls from the neighboring towns – like Leominster, Fitchburg, and Ayer, maybe a couple others – would take the bus into Ayer and take taxicabs out to the Snake Pit. It made it very convenient for all of us and most of us had a pretty good time there.

One Saturday the squadron was invited to the city of Boston for a dinner dance—I don't know who arranged this, it was probably the Chamber of Commerce in Boston – they would set us up with the local debutantes for dates. So we all went. As a matter of fact, my future wife came up from Pittsburgh to attend. The affair went fine and we all got back to the base on a Sunday.

Sunday night as usual we went to the Snake Pit. As we walked in, one of the waitresses came up to us and said "You S.O.B.'s" – she didn't say S.O.B., she spoke it right out – she said, "where were you last Saturday night?" We told her we'd been to a party in Boston. She said, "and you didn't let us know so we could put the word out."

She said, "Saturday night there were one hundred ten young ladies here, and none of you. showed up.. Had any of you walked in, I think they would have been raped on the spot." That was the Snake Pit!

About two weeks later I made a call to Pittsburgh and asked Mary Jayne to marry me. She agreed, and I think I told the story about flying there in an SBD. Anyway, we got back to Ayer, Massachusetts and rented a couple of rooms in a farmhouse in Pepperell, NH.

We had dinner with a bunch of the fellows from the squadron, and they said, "Well, we'll see you later, Ed, we're going to the Snake Pit." Mary Jayne kept saying, "let's go to the Snake Pit." I said, "oh, you wouldn't like that, it's just an old roadhouse, everyone's drinking." But this went on a number of days, a number of requests, and finally I said, "Okay, I guess we'll go to the Snake Pit." So that night we went to the Snake Pit. We're sitting there, having drinks and dancing, and Mary Jayne said she wanted to go to the ladies' room. She came back from the ladies' room laughing. I said, "What's so funny?" And she said, "When I was in the ladies' room, I was behind the doors in one of the areas and I could hear everyone speaking." I heard this one girl say, 'hey, do you see who's here tonight, Pappy's here.' (That's me). The other girl said, 'Yeah, I saw him there, that gal he's with has a ring on her finger – do you think he got married?' The other girl said, 'no, not Pappy, he's here with a married woman.'"

We just celebrated our fifty-seventh wedding anniversary, it was in September.

One day, after flying I drove home to the place where Mary Jayne and I were staying, and she came running out to meet me almost in hysterics. I said "what's the problem?" She said, "Our dog" – we'd decided we were going to buy a little dog like Asta in the movies, a little terrier. We went to a store in Pepperell and as usual we didn't pick out a dog, the dog picked us out. The dog was apparently a combination of Saint Bernard and Collie. They raised them in that part of the country for some kind of duty on the farms. Anyway it was just a puppy. We called it "Wave-off". Wave-off was of course what you get when your landing isn't quite right. Anyway, Mary

Jayne was hysterical. I said, "What's wrong?" She said, "our dog, Wave-off, look at him." Wave-off was sitting under the cow in the shade. I said, "What's wrong?" She said, "How can we get him?" I'd worked on a farm for a while, so I knew how placid cows were. I walked over, and picked up the dog.

When we were about to leave, Mary Jayne went to the store and said to the woman running the store, "We're going to be leaving in two days, I just thought I'd say goodbye." And the woman said, "If you don't mind my asking, would you tell me how many babies you have." Mary-Jayne said, "I don't have any babies." The woman said, "But you buy more Pablum than any of our customers." And Mary Jayne said, "Oh, that's what we feed our dog."

10 July:

Bombed airfields around Tokyo. Lost no pilots. Flew 210 sorties (Air group flew 210 missions that means there were 210 individual flights, which also means some of us flew twice on July 10th. Each flight was ay least 4 hours long.)

14 July:

Strikes on Northern Honshu and Hokkaido. Sunk 7 ferry boats. These were large ships that carried trains from Northern Honshu to the main island of Japan. The ferryboats were not armed. It was like gunnery practice. If your dive was not on target, no drop was made; you just went around and made another dive. This had to make a giant break in the supply chain for Japanese defenses.

15-22 July:

Further strikes on Northern Honshu. Eight of our planes hit by AA. Now working on Tokyo again. Dave Horton and one bomber pilot killed.

24 July:

Strikes on Kuri Harbor. Bombed a Japanese Aircraft Carrier and a Cruiser. The flack from the ships and shore batteries was very heavy. To explain our bombing: We never dropped from a high altitude. We dove on the target until we were about 100 yards above it, released the bomb or rocket then pulled out of the dive. We then gained altitude and took evasive action to avoid the anti aircraft fire.

Jeter splashed a Mert (Japanese plane).

This was a particularly long flight. As we were in the landing pattern Coumbe's plane ran out of gas. He landed in the water near the Essex. He was picked up by a destroyer and returned to the Essex. I landed, caught a wire then ran out of gas. The plane had to be pushed forward so that the next plan could land.

25-28 July:

More of the same. Comstock and Reidy downed a Zeke each. We lost one bomber pilot and one F6F pilot (Weisner). Ray Weisner was later found and rescued. Batten, Brocado and Clark each shot down a Jap plane. This brings our total to 226 enemy planes destroyed. Worked over ships in Kure harbor again. The 30,000 th landing was made on the Essex.

29-30 July:

Hit Tokyo again. We were scheduled to strike Korea, but the mission was called off due to a Typhoon in the area. Thanks- Striking Korea meant flying over Japan, the China sea, then returning. Belly tanks of gas would be required. The flight would be at least eight hours long. Not much fun being strapped in a Corsair for that length of time.

4 August:

Glen Wallace's birthday. He spent it flying between Tokyo and Iwo Jima. The Korea deal was on again then cancelled at the last minute.

6 August:

Our strikes today were to be on a city in China. That's right China. We would carry expendable gasoline in a pod beneath our plane. This would permit us to fly to Japan, cross over it and the China Sea. Why would we do this? The scuttlebutt (rumor) was that Admiral Halsey had already sent information for the next day's headlines." Fifth Fleet bombs city in China."

We did not look forward to being strapped into a corsair for 8 hours.

The missions were scrapped. There were to be no flights today. The reason-The atomic bomb was to be dropped on Hiroshima.

There has been much discussion as to whether the bomb should have been dropped. I personally feel it saved many lives. The letter from President Truman to columnist Irv Kupcinet sums it up.

Letter from Truman to Irv Kupcinet, August 5, 1963

HARRY S. TRUMAN
INDEPENDENCE, MISSOURI
August 5, 1963

Dear Kup:

I appreciated most highly your column of July 30th, a copy of which you sent me.

I have been rather careful not to comment on the articles that have been written on the dropping of the bomb for the simple reason that the dropping of the bomb was completely and thoroughly explained in my Memoirs, and it was done to save 125,000 youngsters on the American side and 125,000 on the Japanese side from getting killed and that is what it did. It probably also saved a half million youngsters on both sides from being maimed for life.

You must always remember that people forget, as you said in your column, that the bombing of Pearl Harbor was done while we were at peace with Japan and trying our best to negotiate a treaty with them.

All you have to do is to go out and stand on the keel of the Battleship in Pearl Harbor with the 3,000 youngsters underneath it who had no chance whatever of saving their lives. That is true of two or three other battleships that were sunk in Pearl Harbor. Altogether, there were between 3,000 and 6,000 youngsters killed at that time without any declaration of war. It was plain murder.

I knew what I was doing when I stopped the war that would have killed a half million youngsters on both sides if those bombs had not been dropped. I have no regrets and, under the same circumstances, I would do it again - and this letter is not confidential.

Sincerely yours,

Harry Truman
Mr. Irv Kupcinet
Chicago Sun-Times
Chicago, Illinois

The Atomic Bomb

Nagaski (A-Bomb) 1945	36,000
British Civillians(German Attacks) 1939-1945	62,000
Hiroshima(A-Bomb) 1945	70,000
Tokyo(US Fire Raid) March 1945	83,000
Dresdon (G.B Fire Raid)	100,000

8 August:

Lt. (j.g.) Coumbe Gets Hit

More strikes on Japan. Bucky Harris was killed when a bomb exploded on his plane in mid-air, (proximity fuse failure). One bomber went straight in-no survivors. One F6F and two TBM's ditched. Crew was picked up by a destroyer. Ship under attack all day by Kamikazes. Several shot down. One destroyer hit. Same air plan for tomorrow. No relief in sight. Morale a little ragged. (Saw one man beating his head against a 5-inch gun mount).

Just two days ago our flight surgeon tried to ground the whole squadron claiming we all had battle fatigue. (We were supposed to have gone home on July 1st as our tour of duty was up)

We proceed to Hokkaido Bay, the northern most island of Japan. Here we dove on Japanese ships anchored in the bay. Vern Coumbe and I were the last two to make our dive.

Vern's plane got hit. We saw him hit the water. We also saw him get out of the plane and swim toward shore.

It was raining and there was zero visibility. Three of us started to climb through the rain clouds. In this situation a tight formation is called for. However, when you cannot see your own wing tips, how can you see to fly close?

We drifted apart. After a few minutes I knew I was in a left turn and was in a diving attitude. That is I knew this by the seat of my pants, as they say. Instruments don't have feelings. The horizon instrument showed I was climbing and that the wings were level. The turn and ball indicated the same thing. A quick check of the altimeter confirmed that the plane was climbing. The speed was showing 270 knots well above the stalling speed of about 85 knots. My gut feeling still told me I was diving to the left. Training and good sense told me to forget my gut feeling.

Sixteen thousand feet later the plane pulled above the clouds into bright sunshine. The other two planes were a long way away but we saw each other and joined up.

Two hours later we should be near the fleet. The clouds were still solid. After another twenty minutes we found a small opening in the cloud cover. Diving through it, we got below and could see the fleet in the distance.

Because of the heavy cloud cover and the rain it was dark. The ship would not turn on any lights. The landing signal officer had on a suit That had florescent stripes outlining his body. The paddles he used to direct us were also illuminated. Landing under these conditions were to say the least a bit stressful.

Vern's widow Misty Coumbe wrote the following:

TRANSCRIPT OF NOTES WRITTEN BY ED PAPPERT AND
VERN COUMBE IN AUGUST 1945 AT THE TIME VERN WAS
SHOT DOWN OVER JAPAN:

August 9th, 1945. Russia declares war on Japan. Japan is twice
struck with the powerful new atomic bomb, and Japan proper is
invaded. You didn't know of the invasion – no headlines, no
newscasts, but the homeland was invaded. The landing force
consisted of one man – Lt (jg) V.T. Coumbe, USNR. The invasion
lasted one day and one night.

But let's begin at the proper place – the beginning. It's 11:38
a.m., and the call comes over the squawk box, "Pilots man planes."
There's no big cheering or any sign of excitement, for this is the last
combat hop for Air Group 83. The F4U (Corsair) pilots have long
faces, for two hours earlier Bucky Harris went out for his last combat
mission. Two tours of duty under his belt – his last scheduled flight
on our last strike day. It was his last combat hop. His 1000-lb. bomb
exploded when it was still attached to his plane. Wave the flag for the
superior American airman. Sure, our two fighting squadrons had 226
Jap planes to their credit. But we also had 14 of VBF's 54 pilots
killed.

No one mentions these men; they seem to be forgotten by all, two
days after their deaths. But every pilot thinks of these missing
comrades before he goes to sleep and wonders who will be next. So
as I said, there was no cheering – "hubba, hubba," or go get them – as
there was last March when we concentrated on kills and not on being
killed. So the pilots manned planes, praying they would come back
and set foot in the ready room once more after that last hop.

The propellers spun and the planes took off. Everything worked
like clockwork, for the Essex had been at sea for 18 months and was
the most efficient ship in the fleet. She, too, was heading for home
after this, her last strike day. Our target was Ominato air base in
Mutsu Wan (Bay). Primary importance was placed on shipping.

The Beasts (dive bombers) and Corsairs started to climb, for there was a 14,000-foot front over which we had to climb. The target was 270 miles away – practically no distance for an airplane. Think again, with a full bomb load and flying at the dive-bombers' speed, we would be two hours getting there. Two hours to listen to the engine and know that with each tick of the prop we were getting closer to Japan proper. This was not new to our air group, we all had at least fifteen missions over the homeland, Kyushu, Tokyo, Hokkaido – you name it. All had twenty more over Okinawa, but that never held the terror that the homeland does. There's the target, and what a target. We expected nice transports, an easy hop. No such luck – there in the bay is a cruiser, three DE's (destroyer escorts) and several transports. The AA comes up – not too bad, the shore batteries cannot get our range and the cruiser is not doing much better. "Jr., your division go in after the bombers, we'll precede them," calls out Ham Reidy, our squad commander.

Now the AA is intense and concentrated, for we are directly over the cruiser and she is fighting for her life. I wiggle my wings so Coumbe can tell I'm going to roll over. It's every man for himself now. "Powee,," someone in front of me gets a hit on the fantail. Time to release our bombs and get the hell out of here. Full power and radical maneuvering and we'll be safe. We're almost to the ocean and safety. "Bobcat 305, this is Bobcat 208, I'm going to land in the bay near where the bombs went in." No! – He's too calm; he can't be going to crash land. "This is Bobcat 215, I saw a bomber go in – no survivors – there's a pilot in the bay, he's in his rubber boat." No call sign, who sent the message we don't know. All Bobcat planes rendezvous five miles east of the beach.

"Godson, this is Pap, let's go back and look for Coumbe." Not very good radio procedure, but who cares. After searching the wrong area for twenty minutes we are told to rejoin the flight, as our gas will be short as it is. So back to the ship we go. My God, what will happen to Coumbe, he must be in the bay. He hasn't a chance in the world. If it had to happen, why didn't it happen yesterday, then we could have had a chance to recover him with an OS2U.

We land and go back to the ready room. Why should we have such tough luck? Oh, but no, our troubles are not over. Over the ticker comes work – change in plan – tomorrow is another strike day. Pilots curse, why can't we be relieved? Why can't the Essex be sent back as she was ordered? We have already flown our share – and a little more. We really have the Japs on the go. So yesterday we learn that our air group has just put in ——#—— combat hours, breaking the record for the number of combat hours flown for any air group that has ever flown from an American carrier ship or any other carrier.

No acey-deucy is played, no card games. Everyone is too tired or too disillusioned to stand another's company. Back in the room Clem Wear says, "You know, Pap, we might be able to save Coumbe. If he can get to shore and hide in the bushes tonight, then swim back out into the bay – it can be done." Ham Reidy and Comdr. Utter are sending pleading communiqués to get permission to use a division for rescue work. It has been promised! Ham will take it. Clem is his section leader and knows what it's like to be down. He spent a night in his raft five miles off the coast of Kyushu. Ham found him the next day and he was rescured by a PBM.

"Ring," – there's the phone. It's three forty-five. "Sorry, Pap, you have to fly. I forgot to call you for breakfast. You take off at 0410." Another five-hour hop. The ready room is buzzing with preparations for the flight. After we hit a small airfield we'll go up and look for Coumbe. The rescue hop has been cancelled. Off we go – the usual thing, bombing another Jap airfield. The attack completed, we shove off for Hokkaido bay. "Be careful of the shore batteries and AA from the Des," warns Tripp, the flight leader.

Maybe he stayed in the bay in his rubber boat all night. If he did, he'd be in about the center. Can't see him. We'll keep looking. "I see him, I see him" – a frantic call from Jones who is searching the east shore. "There he is on that rock waving a white handkerchief." Everyone had a new lease on life, and everyone had a slightly different idea on the subject. "Where is he, fly over him and I can get his location," calls Tripp. "I have it marked, I think I'll drop him a raft," calls Bobcat 265. "No, no, stay away from him, you will just give his position away." My gosh, what are they doing? That's Japan proper, don't they know it's where the Japs live. Hell, he's close enough; he could walk to and report in to Ominato Naval Air Base. "This is Bobcat 217, I better drop him a mirror so he can signal." "Stay away from him, don't go near. If we can find him without aid, the rescue group will surely be able to do so." "This is Bobcat 265, he's broken out his raft and is paddling out into the bay."

Tesmine (——can't read——) climbs for altitude and relays the message back to base. Comdr. Utter then moves heaven and earth and gets permission for four OS2Us to go with out fighters to try to affect a rescue.

When Vern's plane was hit there was no time to decide anything, the engine was completely dead. The right oil cooler broke loose, flew into the cockpit, how it got there is still a mystery. It hit Coumbe's arm, then his head; finally it rested in his lap. The water was very close now. This was not new; Coumbe had made a water landing before. In fact, his last hop. His plane ran out of gas after a mission that was a little too long. But then he had four thousand feet to get set for the landing. Now he had about three seconds. Crash! – Just like hitting a brick wall going 85 miles per hour. The shoulder straps saved him again. The plane would float for approx. 45 seconds if he was lucky. First the oil cooler had to be thrown out. It felt like it weighed a ton, but it was out in a matter of seconds – then unhook the straps and phone cord. This time he was going to make sure he had his life raft with him. Once free of the plane the next step was to unhook his chute and inflate his Mae West. There goes the plane, no time to think of that now. There is a CO_2 bottle that does it, the raft is inflating.

The last of our attacking planes leave. It's 2:30. Vern was thinking if they called for a rescue patrol immediately, I could be picked up. Better keep well clear of the beach. Guess I better start paddling, so I don't get washed ashore. It's three-thirty now; better keep on the lookout for planes. Four-thirty. 5:30. Well, I know there won't be any rescue planes now. Gee, I'll bet old Berube (Ensign

Norman Berube) was hoping for OS2U about this time of day. The squadron sure felt badly when they wouldn't launch an OS2U to attempt to save him on account of it being too late in the day.

Well, my prospects are better than his. Surely if I go ashore and turn myself in I'll become a POW. Maybe I'll meet Bouldin (Lt (jg) Jim Bouldin, who was seen crash landing on Japan). Maybe I'll be beheaded. Wish I'd never seen that picture of a Jap beheading an American aviator. Maybe Halsey will change the plans again. Ha ha, boy, that's something – me wishing we'd have another strike day. Gosh, I can't keep struggling against this surf. Well, it's dark now. There's the beach about a hundred yards away. I better go ashore. If I stay out here all night I'll be so weak tomorrow I won't be able to stay awake. Wonder how deep the water is here. Only up to my waist. Why was I struggling so hard to combat the surf?

Well, Japan, here I come. Looks rather deserted around here – no lights, but then again, I guess they have blackouts here too. I'll bet the little Japanese air raid wardens aren't made fun of like the air raid wardens are back home.

NOTE from Misty: (Vern's widow, who typed this and many of the stories)

All of the above narrative was written by hand by Ed Pappert, Vern's roommate and best buddy. There were one or two names I couldn't make out, but others I could recognize because I remember Vern talking about the people. The Japanese Naval Base, which was near to where he was shot down, was called Ominato. I have a rough map which Vern drew of the area where he was shot down, showing the location of the fleet at 270 miles, a possible rescue submarine about 15 miles from the shore, which would require a hike across a neck of land to get to the Pacific Ocean, and indicating himself out in the bay in relation to the naval base.

This is where Lt.(jg) Vern Coumbe was hit wit A.A.

The next portion is a transcript of handwritten notes by Vern:

As the newscasts have it, I am the only pilot that was ever shot down and rescued from the shores of Japan in this war. But something that wasn't mentioned was the fact, which is of paramount interest, that Air Group 83 was the first group ever to affect such a rescue.

Corsairs and Hellcats swept over to take a glimpse, I guessed to see if I still prospered, several times during the morning of the 10th, and then went off in the distance to circle. This gave me a great sense of security. I felt like the newly hatched robin that had fallen from his nest, and my pop and mom were up there ready to take on any offenders.

Up until the time of the attack on the Ominato Naval base, I had been fortunate never to have been hit by AA, not even had the paint scratched. I had been tracked several times very closely, to the point where I thought my next move might be by last.

Well, old man fate caught up with my speedy Corsair shortly after pullout on the freighter transport. I dove a trifle lower than ordinary in an earnest effort for a direct hit. Both Lt. Godson and Lt (jg) Lamprich were off to my left and a little above when I had about completed my recovery. Besides all the miscellaneous AA filling the sky, a 25-mm.-shore battery was having a fine time following Godson and Lamp around the sky. I say, with a very sad tone to my voice, that this AA line of fire was ninety degrees to my line of flight. And right on in altitude. My first impulse told me to pull up and make a sharp right turn, as the book says – which should have thrown them off on both lead and deflection.

There was a startling shudder originating in the starboard wing, and debris was flung about the cockpit. I suddenly felt a great deplorable sinking feeling in my stomach. No! I hadn't been hit, but the engine had been. It just went "psssst." No more power! No more fly! Maybe no more Coumbe!

The instrument panel was having a field day. No oil pressure! No fuel pressure! No manifold pressure or rpms! The gas tank having been punctured was pumping gas overboard like a busted fire hydrant.

All this had happened at about four thousand feet immediately above the naval base. There were two definite things to do. One set a gliding speed and two, head for the center of the bay. It seemed I was flying a helicopter as I was now gliding at between 160 and 140 knots. Hovering over the Jap base as I was, I glanced down and saw all these ugly bright flashes. I couldn't bear to look again. Letting down at this snail's pace I was an easy target for a poor gunner. And could still be blown to kingdom come.

My thoughts reverted again to my engine. I couldn't convince myself that she had turned over for the last time – never again! About three other pilots had chosen to make water landings at the same time. Consequently the air was filled with transmissions. Believing the golden rule the best tactic at the time, I waited it out. And finally sent my secret out over the ether waves to Godson when I was at about two thousand feet. Evidently someone cut the transmission out, as there was no reply. Emitting with another when my turn came – "Bobcat 205 this is Bobcat 208, I am going down south of the target in the bay – over." Even this was not fully received.

And I ended up flying the plane left-handed thirty feet off the deck, mike in my right hand, putting out the word that I was going in at the position where one of our planes had just crashed. This as you might imagine was done with a total disregard to radio procedure. And you can be sure I didn't know if anybody knew just where I was going to land.

NOTE from Misty: This is where the handwritten narrative by Pappert and Coumbe ends. In my own words I can relate some of what happened after that, from the tale that Vern was asked to tell many times once he returned home.

Vern did make the decision after landing in the water and waiting for several hours in his raft to see if there was any possibility of rescue, to paddle into shore. He found a hiding place in some trees, close to a railroad track, which wound around Mutsu Bay. At one time a troop train went by, and he could see Japanese military personnel in the train, but since it was dark he was not seen. Among the things he considered, should he not be rescued, was to hike across the narrow neck of land between the bay and the Pacific Ocean, where he knew there was a submarine stationed about 15 miles out to sea. His thought was that if he could make it across that land, he might somehow be able to get a signal to the sub and possibly be rescued. During the night he buried a ring that he had had made, which had a skull and crossbones on it – his thought being that if he were taken prisoner that would not be a good design to be wearing! Both atomic bombs had been dropped just before this, and he felt sure that any prisoner taken at that time would receive extremely poor treatment.

Apparently some of his transmissions did get through, because the next day he began to see American planes in the sky and it appeared that a rescue might be underway. He signaled his location, and paddled out into the bay again. At one point a pilot dropped a raft to him, but then had the misfortune of diving straight into the bay. Vern did not know then who this was, but later found out that it had been Clem Wear, one of his roommates. When Vern would tell his story and came to this part of the tale, he had a very hard time keeping from breaking down, knowing that Clem had given his life trying to help Vern. And adding to the tragedy was the fact that Clem's wife had either just had their child or was about to – a child that would never know its father.

Several others have written about the subsequent rescue, but I can add a bit from Vern's perspective. When the first OS2U landed and the pilot accidentally hit the throttle, sending him (Lt. Ralph Jacobs) into the water, and the plane scooting across the water, the guns from the Ominato naval base concentrated their fire on it, thinking there were pilots in it. When the second OS2U came down to attempt the rescue, at first the pilot was going to rescue only Jacobs, as there was not really room for two more in the plane. However, Vern hastily climbed aboard and sat on Jacobs' lap, as he had no intention of being left behind. They did make it off okay, although they were being shot at because by that time the Japanese had realized that there was a second plane and directed their fire to it.

Vern was taken to the battleship from which the OS2Us had flown and subsequently transferred back to the Essex, in time for their departure for the States

Ed, since I am sending this long narrative, thought I would also add a bit about what happened to Vern after he returned home. As you know, he and I were married in October 1945, with you as his best man. After a thirty-day leave, he was stationed at Glenview Naval Air Station, not far from Chicago and Lombard, the small suburb we were both from.

In 1948, after three years at Glenview, one of his fellow pilots there had decided to go to Alaska to homestead, and Vern and I decided that we would like to try our hand at such an adventure. I was rather in favor of his getting out of the service, as he had had another close brush with death while ferrying a Hellcat from Glenview to a small field where the plane was to be used for pilot training for civilians. It was a gravel runway, and as he landed a wheel apparently caught and the plane flipped over, burying the cockpit with Vern in it. Fortunately he was dug out and didn't suffer any injuries. But I had been meeting him that day and saw the plane buried in the ground, a rather harrowing experience.

We did go to Alaska, but due to many circumstances did not end up homesteading. But we loved Alaska and decided to make it our home, after several months in a very sparsely inhabited area known as Soldotna. We then moved to Seward, a small port town on the Kenai Peninsula, both obtained jobs there and settled in. Our first two children were born in Seward in what was still the Territory of Alaska. Vern was then transferred to Anchorage with Standard Oil Company, where our third child was born. After a couple of years in Anchorage, it was apparent that he could go no further with Standard unless we were willing to leave Alaska, so he took a job as an officer in a bank in Anchorage.

In February of 1960 Vern was diagnosed with cancer and had surgery in Anchorage. He was then sent to a Veterans Hospital in Portland, Oregon where further surgery was done. The doctors there offered no hope of recovery, but sent him on to the Veterans Research hospital in Chicago, where he received extensive cobalt and radiation treatment. Our fourth child was born in Illinois while he was undergoing treatment. In August 1960 he was discharged from the hospital, they had done all they could for him, the cancer kept moving from one part of his body to another. All this was just before chemotherapy came into play. Had it been available then, he might have survived. We took our 5-week-old baby and the three other children (ages 6, 4 ½ and 1 ½) back to Alaska, where Vern did try to go back to work, but he lived only about six weeks after our return to Anchorage. He died on September 27th, 1960, and was buried at Arlington Cemetery on October 12th.

15 August:

The War Ends

It's 10:A M, Wonder 21 (Vern Coumbe, Glen Wallace and I) is part of a 12-plane group. We are each carrying a 500 lb. bomb. Our target is any ship in the harbor or a factory if no ships are seen.

An enemy plane is to our right and lower than we are. Ham Reidy (our skipper and leader of the flight) dives toward the single engine plane. It appears to be a Zero. Ham makes one pass. The Zero bursts into flames and crashes into the water.

Ham rejoins the group and we proceed up Tokyo Harbor. The radio crackles then we hear "The war is over. Drop your bombs into the ocean and return to the ship."

The group turns and heads back to the Essex. Lower and to our left can be seen two Zeros being chased by six Hellcats. Both Zeros are splashed. Glenn comes over the air and says "Don't those guys know the war is over?"

We are now in the landing pattern. The prep Charlie is now a Charlie. (This means prepare to land then land) No one is given a wave off) all of us land on the first pass.

16 August:

Wonder 21 is again part of a group of 12 Corsairs flying over the Tokyo area. A flight before us told us of paintings on rooftops asking for food, cigarettes and news. The cooks make up bags of groceries that we carry in the cockpit to drop to the prisoners of war. Flying low over the buildings we see one rooftop with the words VF 83. We fly as slowly as we dare and drop the bags of food and news releases prepared by the ships personnel

A few days later we received the following letter.

CPL. ROY DANDRIDGE
1ST Bn. Middlesex Regt.
British Army

To Officers and Men U.S.S. ESSEX:

I should have written this letter to you some days ago, but owing to the rate of movement and excitement of getting out of Japan, I had no time. I am an ex-P.W. from Camp No. 1 B Tokyo, and I am writing this letter in appreciation for the things you boys did for the men in that camp.

We shall never forget the V.F. 83rd (the Fighting 83rd). They were the first planes to find the camp and from then onward, they did all in their power to make the awaiting of our release, as an enjoyable time as possible. You had us in tears, the first day you came, we were glad to see you. The way you zoomed around the camp, coming in so low, we were afraid you would hit the roof, and did we get a kick out of that. For the cigarettes, candy, gum and books, that you dropped, there are not words in which to express our profound gratitude, all we can say is, "Boys, we thank you from the bottom of our hearts." Of all the receptions I have had in the past month, none will be cherished more in my memory, than your air display over the camp, you certainly raised us up, although our morale had been good all through our P.W. life, 3 years 8 months.

You did great work during the war (you had us a bit scared a couple of times), I would like you to know, the Japs were more afraid of you "Small Boys", than the B-29.
Well, here's to you, may you carry on the good work.

Good luck, and Happy Landings.

Yours Sincerely,

Cpl. Roy Dandridge

The prisoners of war at this site recognized Air Group 83. It may have been from something we dropped them. Anyway it was smart of them as we went back several times. We dropped them food, cigarettes and as they requested news. (note the word "news" in the picture)

During the short existence of Air Group 83, we flew over 10,000 sorties 40,000 flight hours, destroyed 335 enemy aircraft, and sunk 265,00 tons of enemy war ships.

Those of us who survived will never forget the experience. We all like to think we could do it again. In fact, we probably could get those iron birds off the ground, but now "The Landing Would Not Be The Easy Part"

26 August:

Flat-hatting

Flat-hatting (flying very low) is permitted. This is great, the countryside north of the city looks like the northeastern U.S. We are like a bunch of school kids out at recess.

Lt. (jg.) Rosser Clark does not return to the ship. No one seems to know what happened to him.

Two days later Lt. (jg) Clark came aboard. He was brought to the Essex by a small boat. Snuffy (as we called him) said he was just flying around looking at Tokyo when he decided to land so that he could say he set foot on enemy soil. However when he landed he forgot he wouldn't catch a wire with the tail hook. So he damaged the plane. The ground personnel arranged for him to get back to the ship. And it was just in time, one more day and the Essex would have been on it's way to Seattle. Snuffy had some concern about the plane he damaged. Some kind Navy Officer said" forget it, there is so much confusion no one will even ask" He was right no one asked Snuffy what happened to the plane.

27 August:

Wonder 21 is part of a large group of planes that fly over the USS. Missouri. The Japanese are on board turning in their swords. The official surrendering is taking place. Two planes cracked up today on landing.

1 September:

We have been given orders to leave the fleet and return to the states. The Essex has taken over 1000 men to return with us. One rock happy commander came aboard and then turned the ships sprinkling system on flooding us out of our room.

The San Jacinto (sp?), Massachusetts, and the San Diego are with us. Our homeward bound pennant was 1538 ft. long before it broke off and fell into the ocean.

13 September:

Arrived in Seattle, Washington. Home sweet home. Seems strange to approach land without getting shot at.

18 September:

Air group 83 was decommissioned and orders issued to everyone for duty in various places far and wide.

September 1945:

After we arrived in Seattle, Air Group 83 was decommissioned. My decision was to get out of the navy and finish college. My orders were to report to a naval base at Cape May N J and get orders for discharge from there.

When reporting, I was told to see the Admiral. It turned out that he had served on the Essex earlier in the war. He asked about many of the ships personnel. I knew some of them. The Admiral tried to persuade me into staying in the Navy. My plans were to get out of the Navy and finish college.

The Admiral was a likable man. We had a pleasant visit that lasted at least an hour. He wished me well and signed orders for me to report to NAS Atlantic City, N J.

I reported to NAS Atlantic City on a Friday. A high school classmate of mine, Marie Thompson, was stationed at the Atlantic City air station She was in charge of communications.

One of my friends Chuck Dimling asked me to be best man at his wedding. This was to be on the following Monday in Pittsburgh, PA.

I decided to go to Pittsburgh to be best man at Chuck's wedding. Marie said all the orders came through her department via Teletype. When the orders would arrive she would hold them and phone me.

On Sunday I received a phone call from Marie. She said the orders for my transfer to Philadelphia came by mail the same day I left. I was listed as AWOL.(That's Absent Without Leave a punishable offense).

I rushed back to the base at Atlantic City. The commandant of the base said he was going to press charges. Fortunately he had to make the charges and get the approval of the Admiral in Cape May, N J.

The Admiral remembered me. He said, "Forget the whole thing and let the college boy get back to being a student."

Captain Glen and Bonnie Wallace

Retired Captain Glen Wallace writes:

After the Air Group was decommissioned in Sept 1945, I met my wife, Bonnie, in Chicago and saw my year old son, Jimmy, for the first time. When we had his long curly hair cut, Bonnie cried.

Got orders to NAS Atlanta for instrument flight training in SNJs where we learned to do spins "Under the hood" and all that kind of interesting stuff.

Bought a 1937 Packard for $600 and picked up Bonnie and Jimmy in Rockford, Illinois.. Then a six-day trip to NAS Los Alamitos as an Instrument Flight Instructor.

Then I was transferred to NAS Anacostia in Washington, DC as a flight instructor in twin engine SNBs. Completed duty there in 1947. Sold our war bonds and bought a 1941 Buick Convertible for $1500 and Traveled to NAS Atlanta for duty.

Had collateral duty as an Administration Officer and Safety Officer. Flew several different types of planes and had some interesting experiences…

When my buddies were promoted to lieutenant and I wasn't, the Skipper made a trip to Washington to inquire why.. Turns out that due to the fact that I was shot down on Okinawa, my records had been placed in the deceased files.. I was getting paid but not promoted.. The upshot of the whole thing was that I got a letter of apology from the Chief of Naval Personnel and a promotion back dated one year.. The difference in pay was two thousand dollars.

I was assigned to staff duty at NAS Glenview, IL. In 1954 received orders to HS-4, an Anti Submarine Warfare Helicopter Squadron. Took Helicopter training at Pensacola, FL and reported aboard Ream Field Imperial Beach, California.

Went aboard the Aircraft Carrier USS Princeton and flew HSS-1 Helicopters during a six month cruise in the Pacific. This was great duty and we piled up flight hours in the choppers. Flew patrol during the Chinese threat to Okinawa. Returned to State side in 1959.

Four years in the Pentagon, Washington, DC. Got to fly the Presidential back up Helicopters with HMX-1 at Quantico, Virginia. Was part of the team that oversaw production of new aircraft. The P3 Neptune Patrol Aircraft and the A6 attack plane were some of them.. In 1962 my wife, Bonnie, sewed two hundred black arm bands for the Navy men who marched in President Kennedy's funeral procession.

Served two years as Administration and Flight Training Officer at NARTU, NAS Andrews, Washington, DC.. Was promoted to grade of Captain and ordered to duty with the Chief of Naval Air Reserve Training at Glenview, Illinois.

Reported aboard NAS Memphis as Commanding Officer of Naval Air Reserve Training Unit in 1968. My command consisted of 400 Officers and Men and 54 Aircraft of various types.. We won the national combat readiness trophy for being best in the command.

Retired in 1971 and resided in Pensacola, Florida.. Oldest son Jim returned from Viet Nam with Purple Heart.

Youngest son, Jon died at age 25 in 1978 and my wife Bonnie, was buried on our 56th wedding anniversary in 1969.

At 81 years of age, I am still "Milling Around Smartly" and doing retirement things.. Life is good and I am shooting for 110.

Lt. (jg) Vern and Helen (Misty) Coumbe
Circa 1945

Misty and Vern Coumbe

After the War

In October 1945, three weeks after returning from duty on the USS Essex, Vern and Misty were married, with flying buddy Ed Pappert as best man, and several other Air Group 83 buddies in attendance – Wilson, Marcinkoska and Morrissey, all of them elegant in their Navy uniforms.

After his leave and a short honeymoon trip to Southern California, Vern reported to NAS Glenview, for duty in the Operations Department.

In the spring of 1948, Vern came home to report that a comrade at Glenview was resigning and with his family going to Alaska to homestead on the Kenai Peninsula. It took about five minutes for both Vern and Misty to come to the conclusion this might be a great adventure. Vern, now a full Lieutenant, was discharged in July 1948

Vern and Misty headed for Alaska in late November 1949, much to the dismay of families, who were convinced this would be a short-term venture.

Rather than dwell on the early months which were very primitive, we will skip to April of 1950, when the decision was made to move to Seward, a small port town, where Vern was able to find occasional stevedoring jobs, and Misty found work at the TB Sanatorium, and later with the Bureau of Public Roads, which was working on the road to Anchorage. Vern found a job with Standard Oil Company, where there was a tank farm providing petroleum product from the port via the Alaska Railroad to much of Alaska.

In June 1954 the first child was born, son Michael.

In 1955 Vern was promoted and transferred to Anchorage with Standard Oil, and in October 1955 the second child, daughter Melissa was born, also in Seward.

Both Mike and Melissa were born in the Territory of Alaska, somewhat of a distinction since Alaska was still not a State. The move to Anchorage was accomplished shortly after Melissa's birth.

After a time it became apparent that if Vern was to continue advancing with Standard Oil, it would mean a transfer to "Outside," (everywhere in the lower 48).

Vern was offered a job as an officer for the First National Bank of Anchorage. The decision was made to leave Standard Oil and accept this offer so that we could remain in Alaska, where by this time they wished to continue our lives.

A third child, daughter Jennifer was born in April of 1959, and life seemed to be progressing wonderfully.

In February 1960, disaster struck. On the same day that Misty confirmed that she was four months pregnant with their fourth child, Vern's visit to a physician resulted in a probably diagnosis of testicular cancer. Surgery was performed, but the doctor felt that further treatment was indicated, so Vern was sent to the VA hospital in Portland, Oregon.

The doctors informed Misty that Vern had a very short time to live, but they advised sending him to the VA Research Center in Chicago, for further x-ray and cobalt treatment.

While in Chicago their fourth child, daughter Rebecca was born on July 1960.

Vern was discharged from treatment. It was his desire to return to Alaska, which was accomplished in August. Vern attempted to return to work, but became unable finally to stay at work. On September 27, 1960, he passed away.

By now Vern had been advanced to Lieutenant Commander in the Naval Reserve. He was buried on October 12th with full military honors at Arlington Cemetery in Washington, D.C.

1943 Mary Jayne Brine and Cadet Edward Pappert

1944 Ensign Edward and Mrs. Edward Pappert

After the war:

Mary Jayne and Ed Pappert

After coming close to receiving a court marshal for being AWOL at NAS Atlantic City, Ed was given orders to Philadelphia. The discharging procedure there was accomplished in one day.

Ed and Mary Jayne both attended classes at Penn State.

Their first son, Eddie, was born January 18,1947. He is now a Federal Judge. Eddie graduated from Law School at The University of Illinois. He and his wife Marta both graduated from Northwestern University. They live in the Chicago area.

. In June of that year Ed graduated from Penn State and got a job with United States Gypsum Co in Harrisburg PA.

From Harrisburg they moved to Pittsburgh then to Youngstown, Ohio, where daughter Margie was born.

Margie and her husband Chris both graduated from The University of Southern California. Chris was first in his class at the Law School. He is now a partner in the law firm of O'Melvany and Meyers. They and their two boys Sean 15 and Patrick 13 live in Encino, CA.

Fourteen years after Margie was born Mary Jayne gave birth to son Robert. Bobby as he is now called (southern influence) graduated from Pepperdine University at Malibu, CA. He and his wife Lori are both practicing dentists in Charlotte, NC. They met at the Medical University of South Carolina in Charleston, SC.

Ed worked for United States Gypsum for 37 years. For the last 10 years he was VP and general Manager of The Central Products Division.

Ed retired in 1985. They built Mary Jayne's dream house on ocean front property on Hilton Head Island. For fourteen years they enjoyed golf, fishing and watching the Dolphins swim by from their breakfast room windows, They now live near Bobby and Lori in Charlotte, N.C.

THE SECRETARY OF THE NAVY

WASHINGTON

The President of the United States takes pleasure
in presenting the GOLD STAR in lieu of the Sixth Air Medal to

LIEUTENANT, JUNIOR GRADE, EDWARD PAPPERT
UNITED STATES NAVAL RESERVE

for service as set forth in the following

CITATION:

"For meritorious achievement in aerial flight as
Pilot of a Fighter Plane in Carrier-based Bombing Fighting Squadron EIGHTY THREE in action against enemy Japanese forces in the vicinity of Nansei Shoto and Kyushu,
Japan, from March 23 to May 20, 1945. Completing his
thirtieth mission during this period, Lieutenant, Junior
Grade, Pappert inflicted extensive damage on hostile
airfields and installations. His skilled airmanship and
devotion to duty were in keeping with the highest traditions of the United States Naval Service."

For the President,

James Forrestal

Secretary of the Navy

THE SECRETARY OF THE NAVY
WASHINGTON

The President of the United States takes
pleasure in presenting the DISTINGUISHED FLYING CROSS to

LIEUTENANT, JUNIOR GRADE, EDWARD PAPPERT
UNITED STATES NAVAL RESERVE

for service as set forth in the following

CITATION:

"For heroism and extraordinary achievement in
aerial flight as Pilot of a Bomber-Fighter Plane
in Bombing-Fighting Squadron EIGHTY THREE, attached
to the U.S.S. ESSEX, in action against enemy Japanese forces in the vicinity of the Japanese Homeland and adjacent island chains, from March 23 to
April 20, 1945. Completing his twentieth strike
during this period, Lieutenant, Junior Grade,
Pappert inflicted severe damage on enemy airfields
and installations. His courage and devotion to
duty were in keeping with the highest traditions
of the United States Naval Service."

For the President,

James Forrestal

Secretary of the Navy

THE SECRETARY OF THE NAVY

WASHINGTON

     The President of the United States takes pleasure in presenting the SILVER STAR MEDAL to

LIEUTENANT, JUNIOR GRADE, EDWARD PAPPERT
UNITED STATES NAVAL RESERVE

for service as set forth in the following

CITATION:

     "For conspicuous gallantry and intrepidity as Pilot of a Fighter Bomber Plane in Bombing Fighting Squadron EIGHTY THREE, attached to the U.S.S. ESSEX, in action against enemy Japanese forces in Mutsu Wan, Honshu, Japan on August 9, 1945. Skillfully piloting his aircraft in a bombing attack on an enemy cruiser, Lieutenant, Junior Grade, Pappert courageously dived through the intense and accurate antiaircraft fire to score a direct hit with his bomb, thereby contributing materially to the damaging of the enemy vessel. His airmanship and gallant devotion to duty were in keeping with the highest traditions of the United States Naval Service."

For the President,

James Forrestal

Secretary of the Navy

THIS BOOK IS DEDICATED TO THOSE MEN OF AIR GROUP 83 WHO DID NOT COME BACK

Ens. Paul Bacci, USNR

Ens. James M. Barnes
Lt. Cmdr. David R. Berry
Ens. Norman J. Berube, USNR
Lt.(jg) James A. Boatright,
Ens. Paul O. Coburn, USNR
Ens. Robert J. Fahey, USNR
2nd LT. John L. Garlock, USMCR
Lt.(jg) William F. Garner,
Lt. (jg) George A. Gibbs,
Lt. Cmdr. Henry F. Graham, USN
Ens. Denis Gray, USNR
Lt. William H. Harris, USNR
Lt. David Horton, USNR

Ens. Robert M. Jones, USNR
Ens. John L. Kaernan, USNR

Ens. John K. King, USNR
Lt.(jg) Walter J. Lahey, USNR
Lt.(jg) Winston J. Lay, USN
Lt.(jg) Robert H. Moon, USNR
Lt. William A. Rach, USNR
Lt.(jg) Thomas D. Samaras,

Lt. (jg) Warren G. Sigman,

Ens. Grant A. Smith,
Ens. William K. Somers,
Lt. John Spotts,
Lt. James J. Stevens,
Lt.(jg) Sheldon C. Swensen,
Ens. Richard C. Tarlton,
En. Arthur L. Thomas,

Lt. (jg) Clinton E. Wear, USNR
Lt.(jg) Donald L. Willis, USNR
Theodore R. Barry, ARM3c,

Peter Demianchyk, ARM3c,
William M. Driscoll, ARM3c
Joseph M. Eardley, ACRM, USN
Lawrence R. Fowler, AMM2c
Arne W. Lorentzen, ARM1c, USN
Robert J. Melinsky, ARM3c,
Arthur M. Mctheny, ARM3c,
William E. Parson, ARM2c,
Carl C. Roberson, ARM2c,
Joseph R. Wilson, ARM2c,
William T. Winters, ARM2c,

Ens. Ed Pappert 1943

I hope you enjoyed these stories I can be reached at
Epappert20@AOL.com

About the Author

Ed Pappert was born December 3, 1920 in Pittsburgh, PA. He grew up in Dormont, a suburb of Pittsburgh. He became a wrestler. In his senior year he won the Western Pennsylvania Athletic Conference at his weight division.

After high school Ed worked at U.S. Steel in the metallurgical lab. He worked from 11P.M. till 7 A.M. and attended classes at Carnegie Tech (now Carnegie Mellon) during the day. His wife Mary Jayne says the war saved his life as he fell asleep twice while driving back to school after working all night.

Ed applied for and was accepted in the V5 program. This led to his becoming a pilot and an Ensign in the U.S. Navy on December 17, 1943. He qualified as a fighter pilot.

Air Group 83 was formed at Atlantic City, NJ. Ed was part of the fighter squadron flying The Hellcat (F6F). Air Group 83 trained at Ayer, Massachusetts. He and a friend flew an old SBD (dive bomber) to Pittsburgh where he married his sweetheart on September 11, 1944. The air group continued their training on Maui, Hawaiian Islands. On Maui his division switched to flying "the Corsair".

On March 11, 1945 Air Group 83 boarded the Aircraft Carrier "The Essex". Their tour of duty should have been up in June, however they were not relieved. They stayed through the end of the war.

After the war Ed finished his college at Penn State University. He took a job with United States Gypsum Co. He worked for USG for 37 years attaining the position of V P and General Manager of the companies largest division.

Ed and his wife Mary Jayne have three children. They retired to Hilton Head Island. After living there for 14 years they moved to their present home in Charlotte, N C.